What people are saying about

Quiet Courage

I did enjoy looking through ...usly well written. And I was transported to In ...ving touched down there myself... Your vision and love of India run like a clear thread through your writing – but beyond that, your spiritual longing and awakening deepen and enhance this important work.
Stephanie Sorrel, author of *Depression as a Spiritual Journey*

In this book, Philip asks some cogent and searching questions... There is no arrogant attempt to answer these questions in a prescribed way, but Philip lights for us all a candle in the darkness...

With breath-taking honesty, the author describes the spectres that have arisen in his own life and how by embracing them, he has learnt to live in a better way – with integrity...

The sign of a good book is the need to keep recording sentences and paragraphs from it. With this book, I can guarantee that you will need to keep your notepad or your pen close by. It is true to say that I failed to get past even one page without jotting down something that struck me as important... For me, a central point was how a sensitive soul found that through an essentially positive attitude, he was able to turn even the darkest periods into grist for the mill – and moreover realised that the darkest periods are the very things that progress our development and enable us increasingly to become forces for good in the world... It is a story of triumph.
Elizabeth Medler, former Editor of 'New Vision', founded as 'The Science of Thought Review'.

The author says this book is 'written most especially perhaps for those who are teetering on the brink of a hesitant spiritual commitment, or who feel convinced they have no faith at all to turn to – and have no idea either where to find any'.

And indeed, he offers many pointers to living a life of integrity and the cultivation of the inner being, from which 'every jot of kindness counts in a world inclined to cruelty'.

Reading Philip Pegler's work, puts me in the mood of a ramble through spiritual woods on the way to Thoreau's Walden Pond – as his writing has a similar flavour, with his well-chosen words and the eloquent phraseology in this gentle and heart-warming book.

Muz Murray, Spiritual teacher and author of *Seeking the Master – a guide to the ashrams of India and Nepal.*

This review of your life and the truths you have realized, as a result of its most traumatic moments, reflects your message of the need for integrity – that is to be straightforward and trustworthy. Although you say that 'words can never do justice to the living truth,' you have opened your heart to try to do so. Even if you have not managed to capture the living truth in its entirety, its essence shines through the book – nevertheless.

For me, the early death of your mother and your love of her glow at the heart of this book; and your evocation of this in your depiction of your memory of her... is as beautiful as it is heart-rending... that you have spent your life searching for its deeper meanings, is a tribute to her, I feel.

This book stands as testament to your search for meaning in the face of the vicissitudes we all face in differing ways – and of our own mortality. I have found much in it to stimulate and encourage me – thank you for that.

Charles Becker, Psychotherapist and author

There is no greater mystery than this: Ourselves being the Reality, we seek to gain reality. We think that there is something hiding our Reality and that it must be destroyed before the Reality is gained. That is ridiculous. The day will dawn when you yourself will laugh at your past efforts. That, which will be on the day you laugh, is also here and now...
Sri Ramana Maharshi, Indian sage, (1879–1950)

The divine creed is a creed of living experience. Talking alone is not enough – application is the main requirement.

One day Love will stand above everything. It will wipe out all defects. It is the only power that sets everything to rights. Leave everything to love...
Peter Deunov, Christian teacher of the Perennial Wisdom, (1864–1944)

Quiet Courage of the Inner Light

Finding faith and fortitude in an age of anxiety

Quiet Courage of the Inner Light

Finding faith and fortitude in an age of anxiety

Philip Pegler

CHRISTIAN ALTERNATIVE
BOOKS

Winchester, UK
Washington, USA

JOHN HUNT PUBLISHING

First published by Christian Alternative Books, 2020
Christian Alternative Books is an imprint of John Hunt Publishing Ltd.,
No. 3 East St., Alresford, Hampshire SO24 9EE, UK
office@jhpbooks.com
www.johnhuntpublishing.com
www.christian-alternative.com

For distributor details and how to order please visit the 'Ordering' section on our website.

Text copyright: Philip Pegler 2018

ISBN: 978 1 78904 345 7
978 1 78904 346 4 (ebook)
Library of Congress Control Number: 2019933924

A CIP catalogue record for this book is available from the British Library.

Design: Stuart Davies

UK: Printed and bound by CPI Group (UK) Ltd, Croydon, CR0 4YY
US: Printed and bound by Thomson-Shore, 7300 West Joy Road, Dexter, MI 48130

We operate a distinctive and ethical publishing philosophy in all areas of our business, from our global network of authors to production and worldwide distribution.

Contents

Other books by the same author:
Hidden Beauty of the Commonplace
Meeting Evil with Mercy
Peace is the Path – Love is the Law
(An unpublished account of Indian travels)

Mysterious and majestic – the sacred hill of Arunachala.

This book is offered to my close companion,
Wendy – with love as ever.
It is also dedicated to the memory of our
dear friend, Ursula,
who sadly has not lived to read it in the light of day.

Foreword

In his book *Quiet Courage of the Inner Light*, author Philip Pegler writes of what he has lived through and what he discovers in the present moment.

When he mentions an Indian festival, which includes entering a walk around a sacred hill, it seems like an invitation to join him. The pilgrimage walk becomes an investigation into what might sustain us – bring us fortitude – through difficulties and uncertainties in life.

This investigation is characterized by clear vision, by an undoubtedly authentic inner experience, which is steeped in Indian spiritual teaching but translated into everyday language.

The truth about our identity, the author suggests, is not for attaining but simply recognizing. Day by day, resting in the ground of our being will bring resilience and joy to our lives.

Here is the bedrock.

As a guide Philip Pegler is respectful, sensitive and measured. We will be tested, he warns. Life will place severe demands upon us. His own trials, shared with candour, lead him to assure us that turmoil can teach us tenacity and eventually bring fresh perspectives.

The ground of our being is never completely lost. In returning to it in the present moment, we will find communion with everyone and a natural empathy.

This book is presented with the deepest conviction and goodwill.

As a very fine distillation of wisdom, it celebrates and honours who we really are.

Colin Oliver
Nature poet and author of *Incredible Countries: Selected Poems*

Preface

Bearer of Light

The path is anywhere and everywhere. It is life itself. It is the wind blowing through the window, the blackbird singing on top of the tree. It is within our struggle for expression as we reach out for affection or understanding, on our knees in prayer, through our stumbling words, our sorrows and our joys.

The life of God within us is always pressing for release, so it would seem there is no need to choose any one path more than another. This is the boundless embrace of Being, which alone has the power to change our outlook as it bestows a clear vision of the way ahead.

Poetry often seems to work better than prose in conveying the essence of sublime spiritual qualities that are ineffable and so beyond the bounds of ordinary language. Yet there are exceptions to every rule and to my mind, the passage that introduces these introductory comments is a good example of just how powerful lyrical prose can prove to be in expressing the inexpressible.

The words I have quoted here were written by the sensitive Nature writer, Clare Cameron, who became a valued mentor to me in my youth, after I first encountered her writings during my years in India. She was the subject of a biographical study I wrote a few years ago, entitled 'Hidden Beauty of the Commonplace'.

It was a task that taught me much as I undertook it – and I often return to those reflections on her quietly exuberant life, because in their penetrating clarity they never fail to remind me of the essential truths I continually seek to articulate in my own written work.

Clare was for many years the Editor of a small but influential Christian magazine, dedicated to comparative religion and positive thinking. In that role as spiritual guide – and through her own contributions to 'The Science of Thought Review' – she saw it as her duty to awaken her readers to a more enlightened way of facing adversity, both within themselves and in the troubled outer world.

She perceived things as they truly are in their totality – and not as divided fragments. Her expansive world-view inspired her many admirers, helping them make more sense of the suffering, which is an intrinsic part of human existence – never something to be evaded but utilised instead as an invaluable element of the spiritual journey.

Clare wrote with persuasive conviction in her monthly editorials of the profound truths of the universe, but for me her most meaningful teaching was conveyed in a kindly silence by her unassuming, personal example as a supportive friend.

She sowed the seeds of wisdom within my youthful, aspiring mind with mindful care, but the subtle insights she communicated upon my return to England, have only unfolded their most profound meaning gradually. They have done so quietly and in their own good time – like delicate plants opening to the warmth of the sun.

What people need most, she realised, was not the patchwork repair of worn-out notions, but the introduction of an entirely new paradigm – an altogether fresh way of seeing. She sought to convey a creative attitude towards living – to awaken a conscious awareness of the spirit of truth within everything; she never permitted one to be content with the mere letter which often carries so little real meaning.

Without saying so in as many words, Clare charged me with the responsibility of standing on the threshold as a bearer of light in my own turn – in my own measure, able and willing to pass on to others from hard-won experience what I now know for myself about spiritual practice in daily life.

To be a bearer of light is simply to make way for the essence of life – always silently present in the background – to shine forth. To be attentive to that True Light – ever quietly waiting to be revealed as the ground of being within oneself – is to encourage others to avail themselves of the same inner Light, as shown to them.

We can then share with one another the good news about Love, Truth and Beauty, as we ourselves have understood those universal qualities. We do so by quiet example – but never by dictate, for such would be coercion, which is nothing short of violence. Where is true love to be found in that?

* * *

World problems have become much more complex and acute in the 35 years since Clare Cameron died at the age of 86. In the meantime, the challenge of communicating effectively those universal spiritual principles that make for peace and harmony, remains as urgent as ever – and will inevitably do so, while mankind's yearning for relief from suffering remains unassuaged.

In a long life of tireless creativity, Clare never ceased to uphold the sanctity of existence, while affirming the essential goodness of all human beings without exception – notwithstanding the foolishness and vice to which mankind in its ignorance is heir.

Anyone seriously wishing to follow in her courageous footsteps will find in her writings unfailing encouragement to do so. A further brief extract from the work of this gifted Nature mystic is not out of place here, because it sets just the right tone for my own book, while offering an evocative glimpse of a noble and liberating attitude to living:

Let me stand for peace and order in a disordered world. Let me not be involved in the feverish distractions – the constant busyness and restlessness that drives so many lives – but tune my days and nights to the quiet rhythms of the universe. For these express and satisfy the spirit.

Let me find my personal rhythm in that Greater Rhythm, and abide in it in all changing scenes, circumstances and events, as a ship rides the sea or a bird the air. For this is to feel one with, and at home in the universe which nourishes, sustains and for ever recreates us through life and death...

Philip Pegler
Midhurst, West Sussex. 5 January, 2019
www.hiddenbeautyoflife.com

Prologue

The Far Shore

The summit of Arunachala – glimpsed from the ashram far below.

*Ah! What a wonder! It stands as an insentient Hill. Its action is
mysterious, past human understanding. From the age of innocence,
it had shone within my mind that Arunachala was something of
surpassing grandeur... When it drew me up to it, stilling my mind,
and I came close, I saw it stand unmoving.*
Sri Ramana Maharshi

In the cool and fragrant air of early morning, there was no doubt whatever in my mind. I was back – enveloped once again in the extraordinary and vibrant consciousness, which signifies India. There is nothing quite like that dynamic atmosphere of heat, dust and bright light – and precisely the same perception held true, as far as I was concerned, regarding the astonishing scene, which greeted my eyes at this early hour before the burning sun ascended.

Before me stretched a broad and surging river – a steadily flowing current, made up not of drops of water, but of a multitude of Hindu pilgrims in colourful garb, who were all making their determined way around the eight-mile perimeter of an ancient, rugged hill, long held as sacred.

This was an impressive demonstration of faith by any stretch of the imagination – a grand display of unswerving faith in the power of blessing, which was vested, on this special feast day, in the resplendent form of the great Lord Siva, whose embodiment as the hill of Arunachala, was due to be celebrated that very evening with the kindling of a flaming beacon on its summit.

In former days, when I used to walk this way often, it would have taken just a few moments to cross the road that led to the famous ashram of Sri Ramana Maharshi, where I had lived on and off for years. But not now – not today on 2 December, 2017 as the great annual feast of *Deepam* approached its culmination.

This morning, I would need to leave all my Western reservations well behind me if I wanted to cross to the other bank of that vast river of humanity – if I really wanted to reach the far shore where true faith resides.

I hesitated tentatively for a moment, but a final decision was hardly in doubt as I plunged in to mingle with the devout crowd of pilgrims – each one of them buoyed up by the immense energy of this remorseless current.

It was as if I had become a walker in a new world in this vast throng, a keen observer careful not to miss the least detail of sensation, or the merest encounter of eye or hand in the jostling movement of everyone on the path around the hill.

I knew in those moments only one thing for sure: Here was certainly home from home and where a good part of me still belonged – intent on tracking down the truth of my soul in the quest for Self-knowledge.

I was acutely aware that it was here in India long ago that I had taken my first tentative steps on the spiritual path. Now it was in this sacred land, nearly fifty years later, where I was being offered the rare opportunity to reflect upon the passage of the years in between – years spent mostly far away in the land of my birth in England.

I had seen some hard times for sure in a vivid life that had encompassed a great deal, but which had seemed to rush by in a trice. Perhaps this would be the most auspicious place to pause for a while and begin framing some of my most poignant memories and reflections with clarity and in all candour. I could but try anyway – it certainly seemed a task well worth attempting.

In quest of wisdom – the author and another young Western devotee with an Indian holy man in 1970, following *Darshan*.

Part One

Background to Awakening

1

A Faith with No Name

It may need just a small gesture of faith – an honest attempt to surrender self-will at the start of a new venture. Then, when the task of writing is offered up to the immediacy of present experience, seemingly from nowhere can occur the closing of a crucial gap between intention and action.

We have no idea just how it has happened, but suddenly our faltering attempts to communicate are rewarded as our creative energy goes full circle – and we find the flow. A broken circuit seems to have been restored, so that the words and ideas flow with far less hindrance. At last we feel unified with an incisive clarity that speaks of joy.

For once we know quite clearly what we need to say in the here and the now and we can express it more succinctly too – simply because we are at one with what we are doing. I feel firmly that this is how any book on practical spirituality needs to be written nowadays if it is to prove effective in conveying a dynamic message of hope and reassurance to a troubled world.

And that is also how personal life should be conducted with integrity. It should be lived in strength and dignity within the greater light of the totality of the universe, as we begin to recognise that we are not separate from ultimate reality – and never have been.

Such recognition is immensely important, for it is the sense of alienation from oneself and others that causes the greatest suffering – and nowadays this gulf of loneliness and distrust urgently needs to be bridged by far greater understanding and compassion.

There is a precious secret well hidden in the present moment, you see – and we will need to come upon this wondrous discovery of oneness eventually, if ever we wish to be truly satisfied with the life we are living.

Unless we ourselves are established in some degree of deeper and more harmonious understanding, we can never hope to be of real service to the wider community, so often afflicted by uncertainty and turmoil. Yet when we do happen upon this transformative mystery of the One in the many, we will at least be enabled to point out the way to that profound insight that can bring release from conflict and an enduring sense of peace.

The rest is up to the reader, one might say, but only to some extent – because effort can only go so far; the eternal presence ever exists at the heart of our being but can never be grasped by dint of striving.

Awareness of the presence of God comes by what is usually known as Grace, but the action of that grace is mysterious – past human understanding. Perhaps it is best to speak mainly of receptivity – to suggest that the ineffable divinity is drawn to us by heartfelt sincerity, but only perhaps when we are open and ready to receive Its gifts.

Courageous integrity is the light that leads us on, before finally revealing the hidden doorway into the depths of our true nature. It is then that firm faith in Supreme Reality begins to form and take root within us – and this conviction that we are on the track of truth will provide the strength necessary to encounter darkness and turbulence in the outer world.

Enough strength to cope with our responsibilities always comes just when we need it, provided we remember that negativity in its manifold forms is an important part of existence which we have no right to evade. We are an expression of the world in all its beauty and sorrow – and have a duty of care towards the earth upon which we live.

It is no small privilege to be able to knowingly fulfil this duty as a citizen of the world – pointless as it may seem in a worldly sense for most ordinary individuals with little influence to wield.

Our own contribution may appear to us to be insignificant, but every jot of kindness counts in a world inclined to cruelty – every positive gesture is of value in a society so accustomed to place emphasis on what is negative. It is vital that we reflect on these things at the outset.

* * *

This book is concerned with the nurturing of courage and the exercise of higher reasoning, but it is also all about genuine faith – written for those people who need courage and faith most of all. It is a work written most especially perhaps for those who are teetering on the brink of a hesitant spiritual commitment, or who feel convinced they have no faith at all to turn to – and have no idea either where to find any.

I want to reassure any readers who find it difficult to trust in a supreme power, which they cannot visualise, that the kind of universal faith I have in mind is entirely natural. It is a faith already inherent within them and does not need to be made. It insists upon the use of no particular name to cause division or offence, although it answers to many beautiful names – God, Truth, Reality or Love amongst them.

Such universal faith is utterly non-violent and all-inclusive in its concern. It cannot possibly threaten anyone and belongs to all mankind, yet it cannot be commanded – and therefore it remains free to be of service to anyone who needs it.

I have the deepest respect for anybody of any colour, creed or culture who ventures to give courageous expression to an authentic faith of this kind – for they are the light of the world.

When you abide in such a profound faith, you yourself become open to receive wise and reliable guidance from the source of your own being. You may be sure then that genuine spiritual guidance from within will lead you unerringly to the supreme love, which will forever keep you enfolded in safety.

That great love too is inside oneself – a jewel to be cherished – but only when we continually celebrate its beauty, may it become our constant companion.

When all is said and done, this is a book that dares to consider and thus honour the very essence of life, while leaving dogma and creed largely aside – just for now. To honour spiritual essence is to bear witness to the Greater Life within our mundane affairs; it is to aspire to approach that great mystery, which is transcendent, through the immanence of all created things in their wonderful multiplicity.

When through prayer and reflection we draw near to our own soul, we find the deep truth we really need is already there to welcome us.

2

The Source of all Virtue

What is authentic spirituality – and what noble qualities are needed so we may stand up for what is truly sacred in today's dangerous, divided and often sceptical world?

As it celebrates the true worth of courage, this book faithfully records some significant keynotes of this author's lifelong spiritual quest – and reflects upon the joys, sorrows and profound lessons to be learnt on the challenging path to the ground of being.

At the very centre of the work, lies an essential paradox – the most poignant of conclusions. It is within the anguished darkness of tragedy or disaster, that so often the clear light of fortitude is kindled. And it is beneath the lengthening shadows of doubt and desolation that you may find the hidden doorway to the deepest reality.

Sound solutions to the intractable problems of our age abound in the perennial wisdom that has come down to us over the centuries, but the wisest of answers will prove unavailing without education of the heart and illumination of the mind.

It is through the natural intelligence that arises with deep understanding, that we come to recognise our true nature as the universal consciousness that can never really be lost – because it is the source of everything. And it is also through this deeper intelligence that eventually – with illumined understanding – we will be enabled to resolve not only our personal problems, but those of the wider world also.

This then will be the most fundamental discovery we can make – the dawning of a grounded knowledge that is simple and steady and available to one and all.

The pivotal realisation that is outlined in this study concerns nothing else but our own consciousness. This simple awareness of being alive, which we have been graciously granted even without asking for it, is the most precious gift we could ever receive – and it is the source of all virtue.

All consciousness requires to come to fruition as an awareness of overflowing abundance in our experience is the recognition of its primary importance in our life. Consciousness is already whole and entire within us and does not have to be made, attained or improved. We are already complete with no missing parts – and at one with the universe. Consciousness is not simply something we *have* – it is what we *are* in our essence. It is our real nature.

While the world is beside itself in crisis – when things are falling apart all around us – we just need to take refuge in the aware, still and lucid consciousness that is ever-present at the centre of our own being, and which dwells deeply in the hidden heart of all created life too.

This clear and still centre is where reality truly abides – and it is enough to remember that one fact. So long as we are wide awake in conscious awareness, we remain essentially safe and well, upheld by life itself. There is no reason whatever then to give way to despair, because at the end of the day, despite any amount of doubt or difficulty, we will be blessed by the mysterious, indwelling power that brought us into being – and sustains us still.

3

A Crisis of Perception

The fabric of life forms a fine-spun tapestry of all things, and yet how readily this interwoven wonder of Nature is taken for granted – profoundly precious though it is. It seems grimly ironic – and tragic too – that all too often, the truths most simple and self-evident are the ones most easily ignored and overlooked.

We live in an elemental world, full of hidden marvels and upheld by a delicate balance of natural forces. But heedless of our duty of care, we have all too often squandered the bounty of goodness that the universe offers and have shattered for no good reason the ordered framework that is there to protect us.

We still barely pause to consider the consequences, before we rush in to interfere, brushing aside the inconvenient with impatience, instead of standing by with respect – to watch what is best for the good of all.

That is a counsel of perfection that the world has never wanted to hear – and is still remarkably reluctant to follow. After all, a step too far – foolhardy as it might appear to outside observers – could do vested interests down. The damage that dominant players may inflict on the environment in pursuit of greater wealth and power in the high-tech societies of our day, is of little concern to them and is fully justified, as far as they are concerned – even if it is at the expense of other parties.

Without checks and balances, it is from these sorts of selfish and entrenched attitudes, that corruption soon comes to infect countries and communities that have been rendered most vulnerable by war and deprivation.

And amidst the heedless jostling for position of this kind, the principal aim is usually one and the same – that the strongest participant in any arena of influence should prevail, thereby gaining immediate advantage in the short-term scramble for success. That is the main priority – simply the survival of the fittest, according to the ancient law of the jungle.

Surely there can be no harm in that, just occasionally? At least that is how the usual narrative has gone. But not so much now – not any more – for this selfish version of global affairs will no longer wash when the world is falling apart.

See clearly then how it is power that is cherished most of all, because profit brings power – and power is the chief prize to seize and retain. For love of power, too many leaders still look to the ends of the earth in the arrogant spirit of domination, but they seem rather less inclined to travel the extra mile for the sake of peace. If only more men were wise – and if all leaders loved peace more than power – they would certainly do far more to keep it.

Thirst for power has always been the downfall of dictators – undermined as they usually are eventually, through the corrosive effects of the very power they have seized. But while those same corrupt tyrants hold sway, is it any wonder that the desperate and destitute should flee for refuge to distant parts, where peace may just hang on – unless it has vanished by the time they get there?

There are so many other questions, impossible to answer adequately. Why is the utter futility of war not seen once and for all? How is it acceptable for one huge crisis to follow another, while love counts for nothing and cruel confusion reigns by proxy? It is surely the sad reverse of normality, made all too familiar amidst incessant discord. Is it not possible that the time has really come for mankind to act decisively – and search for the real causes of suffering, before it is too late?

Better by far to ponder these abiding truths of life and death – time and eternity – than languish in despair from suffering self-made. The clearest insights spring from the most painful contradictions within our own situation, while honest contemplation of private truths brings its own reward in integrity and repose. Self-knowledge alone can bring a profound and lasting cure for deep sorrow.

* * *

The world is evidently in crisis – and it is above all an existential crisis of perception. It constitutes a kind of entrenched misunderstanding, related to widespread confusion about human consciousness, the true nature of which has not yet been apprehended by mainstream society.

The ways we have been taught to regard problems – the attitudes underlying our basic approach to the challenges of living – are all too often confrontational, inadequate or misplaced. And this is usually because our conceptions of what represents happiness and success are partial and divisive in their failure to comprehend the totality of life – and to embrace it in practical concern with a mature understanding of its inherent sanctity.

In short, we have forgotten how to find true harmony and ease in life, caught up as we are in busy and stressful occupations, with hardly any time for calm and considered reflection. Contemporary society in the West has largely lost touch with the cultural roots that sustained it in former days. That is the origin of our current troubles, which continue to usher in so much unnecessary hardship.

Something has had to give – and it is the remorseless disintegration of failing structures of power and authority that seems to be taking place. Excessively large and moribund organisations are finally losing credibility, because the arrogant manner by which the resources of the earth have been regarded and managed hitherto is at last being called into question more widely.

The abundance of the earth is not there to be squandered at our selfish discretion; the fertility of the earth does not exist, solely to be exploited in the cause of technological progress, or in the name of endless economic expansion – at any cost. These self-evident truths are becoming ever more broadly acknowledged.

Indeed, the scope and penetration of global media reporting is so great nowadays that you no longer need to be especially clear-sighted to realise that contemporary society has lost its way – and that the world's eco-systems, are more gravely under threat than ever.

Catastrophic conditions on earth beyond imagining surely beckon, if humanity stubbornly refuses to change course towards a sustainable future. It is only a profound shift of attitude in support of a holistic world-view – and a decisive return to a sane and balanced reverence for all life – that can accomplish this.

A wholesale regeneration of the environment and the re-appraisal of moral imperatives are urgent tasks that can no longer be postponed. The challenges ahead are immensely daunting and yet there is still good reason for hope.

The noble aspiration to restore global harmony on all levels is now at the heart of a wholesome grassroots movement, which will accept nothing less than a radical change in perspective that can embrace global issues in the light of oneness.

When you look at the plight of humanity with the eyes of clarity and compassion, the world is made new for you – and your own vision of wholeness will encourage other people of goodwill to follow in your example. Maybe this is the only way by which enduring harmony and peace can ever become established on earth.

4

The Inner Ground of Meaning

For each one of us, our life so full of early promise, can easily become a maze from which one struggles to extricate oneself – a distinct puzzle we are obliged to solve. But to begin with, prompted by some obscure intuition, we can only guess whether by good fortune Life itself may see fit to supply us with the hidden key to the riddle of who or what we really are – and may be destined to become.

It helps a great deal when we realise that, underlying everything we attempt, is a deep search for meaning. This quest for authentic meaning in turn gives rise to a dynamic sense of definite purpose, which at least yields some satisfaction if not quite joy. At least it offers tantalising hints of the best direction of travel in search of our unknown destination, where we hope to find fulfilment.

But before long we find we are going deeper. We cannot help but notice somehow that this insistent urge for meaning is linked to the most fundamental requirement of all. This is the pressing need to establish at all costs the essential truth of our being and to make conscious contact with our inner ground of awareness. This alone is where the constancy of true love can be uncovered. We begin to see that now.

If only we can come to *know* who we are, then perhaps we can learn to *be* who we are knowingly. Maybe that is the primary reason for having been born and the only reliable way to find abiding happiness.

We finally discover that it is the profound love we bear for our own existence, which sustains us best in the face of every kind of difficulty. It is the natural love of life in fact that continually spurs us on despite all manner of obstacles – and it is this that can provide unquenchable hope that everything will turn out for the best in the end somehow, and contrary to all appearances.

* * *

Authentic spirituality endeavours to outline a path that is sane, measured and balanced. It is as wise as it can be in a sceptical age when traditional wisdom has become overtaken by rapid advances in technology and sadly distorted by distrust – if not simply lost in the stress and haste of disregard.

Truth does not need to be attained, but only requires to be recognised – that is the deep understanding we need to come upon and that too is what enlightenment really is. I realise this now, but of course it was certainly not always the case. A long and arduous search has been required for me to appreciate such a simple truth.

Regarding this book – what began with the single intention to outline a unifying vision of harmony and wholeness to serve as a succinct reminder of the most precious teachings I have absorbed, has developed into a much more challenging project.

An attempt has been made to articulate a sane and even-handed approach to matters of faith, which is resilient enough to stand scrutiny in a divided and sceptical world, more inclined than ever to view uniformly restrictive versions of a secular, scientific materialism as the only reality.

Thankfully democracy and human rights are high on the agenda in the West, but capitalism, based on the profit motive and inherently self-seeking, is volatile to say the least and hardly serves to eradicate either injustice or poverty. And modern society's continual preoccupation with political, economic and social concerns – vital as they are – tends to mean sacred matters have often been elbowed aside in disrespect, only to become a big problem, whenever a balanced perspective has got lost.

The gulf of misunderstanding between sacred and secular

viewpoints can only be bridged by reconciliation and a tolerant educational system that supports multicultural diversity. The approach outlined here may be regarded as representing a wholesome, natural spirituality, which deserves to be taken seriously – if only that it may help restore the tarnished credibility of sacred viewpoints within mainstream thinking – understandably still wary of extreme and pernicious, ideology.

Despite the highly-charged atmosphere of public debate surrounding religious and ethical issues nowadays, there does seem to be a growing realisation of the vital importance of inter-faith dialogue. It suggests that a more broad-minded attitude is gaining ground, and this augurs well for a less intolerant and more enlightened future. Yet the very word 'sacred' is still viewed with some suspicion, as it is a bitter reminder of the savage cruelty religious fundamentalism can engender.

The wholesome view that life is inherently sacred in a profound manner transcending religious differences, is certainly not widely held in the West. The prevailing mood by contrast has been one of distrust or misrepresentation of traditional religion, while the sometimes over-arching views of science have tended to hold sway. Meanwhile, people inclined to alternative views of spirituality, have frequently been maligned or dismissed as idealistic.

Until recently, this has been the default position of society, and the balance of opinion is still distinctly tilted towards a secular materialism. It is a world-view that has contributed to a general sense of confusion and has done nothing to reduce stress. We find ourselves living in an age of great anxiety – but it need not be so.

* * *

What is truly sacred can well look after itself, but perhaps it deserves better from a world, which according to religious sensibility at least, owes its very existence to the numinous presence that pervades all and everything. If only a calm reverence for life prevailed everywhere, how much easier it would be for nations to co-operate in combating global issues. How beautiful then the world would become.

Yet notwithstanding the mounting problems that mankind faces, there is still good reason for enduring hope. For one thing – at long last the realms of science and religion are no longer viewed as incompatible. Instead they are seen to blend in an increasingly shared recognition of the profound mystery of the universe.

It is significant too that the greatest of spiritual leaders, scientists and philosophers alike – in courageous exploration of truth wherever it leads – have always transcended arbitrary differences of opinion, to encourage humanity.

Reality has many facets and can be approached from many different angles, but it will always dwell far beyond any attempt to formulate or fix it in any single framework of thought or sentiment – sacred or secular. Words can never do justice to the living truth.

5

Something Quite Magical

When, on the rough road to the still place of wisdom within us, we decisively move in the intangible realm of our intentions away from the arena of warfare towards non-violence and peace instead, the universe responds accordingly. It now seems to protect and sustain us in a mysterious manner, which can neither be logically explained or denied – for it is intangible but also unmistakeable.

The courage derived from this wholesome new attitude to living has somehow introduced an altogether fresh element into our everyday experience – a redemptive quality with the power to transform our outlook. Something that is quite magical can occur when this bravery blends with the simple sense of being aware, with which we are so familiar but normally hardly notice.

The smallest spark will suffice to light a blazing fire to warm and encourage us. Something similar occurs with the addition of the invigorating quality of courage to our existing way of being and knowing. Courage delivers us from hesitancy and opens our vision to an entirely new perspective.

Whereas before one may have felt overwhelmed and weak, now for no apparent reason one feels strong and ready for anything. It is as if instantly one has found a reliable sanctuary to which one can retreat when under pressure.

The relief is enormous. Heartened and suddenly renewed in brave purpose, you hardly recognise yourself from the pale, uncertain shadow you had seemed to be just a few moments earlier. For as soon as your conscious awareness is touched by even a trace of courage, it feels strong and certain – almost impregnable and somehow filled with fresh hope.

The more courage we feel, the more strength there is at our

disposal, and one finds natural abundance everywhere one looks. How could we have possibly missed it before? And the very moment we open-up to courage, in that very instant too we become available to love – to its gentle influence and incredibly uplifting inflow. Then it is Love that acts – and not us. And this is precisely because love and courage are inseparable, two sides of the same coin.

How or why we feel so much better matters not a bit when this love reminds us of its everlasting existence. For when love appears as if from nowhere, we are informed by its mercy and in our own measure can show kindness and compassion to everyone – near or far and whether we know them or not.

When courage finds its voice within us, one thing is certain – our quality of living is transfigured as the ordinary sense of self is penetrated and uplifted by the luminous, indwelling, spirit. That universal life-force is boundless and inherently free – full of a dynamic power and joy.

So, this is what real joy is – but at first the intensity is almost too much for us to bear. And sooner or later anyway, that sense of boundless power will shyly but firmly withdraw until the next time – and that is why progress and inward change must to be so gradual on the spiritual path.

At least it is good that one knows it now, and nothing has been lost. There is certainly no reason for pessimism or doubt after this profound experience, which will be a vivid memory we can never forget.

For once this quiet courage of the inner light has revealed itself to us, we will never be abandoned to despair – even if for the time being awareness of that luminous state seems to have been veiled from view.

The ease and happiness that accompanies the true Light – momentary as our experience of it may have been – is our real condition, and a natural expression of our deepest being, which is inherently pure.

So now the real work of the inward path will begin, but the steep, winding road to Self-knowledge, which had seemed so arduous before, will certainly seem nowhere near as hard.

Even as we look for courage to fight our daily battles, so courage expects us to stand up for our own convictions with all the fortitude we can muster. We will be only too glad to leave our hopes and fears behind, once we learn to allow the hidden action of love to determine the outcome of our affairs.

6

Bedrock of Reality

Abiding and universal – few words are more expressive of profound truth than these two adjectives. And described incisively in such evocative terms as these, we can soon find some searching questions of such significance, that they have the potency to totally turn one's life around.

What is the essence of my existence?

Where do I find my true origin?

What is the nature of being?

Who am I?

These are the sort of simple, existential considerations, that if contemplated in a spirit of keen inquiry, immediately draw one's attention deep within and can give form, purpose and direction to every living moment.

They are the kind of thoughts that have real power to renew our days and nights, whenever we feel lost or disempowered. Questions like these anchor us firmly in the bedrock of reality.

For when you seriously and insistently question your very existence, something cold, hard and opaque in the mind and heart begins to shift and melt.

You begin to observe everything more keenly and see with very different eyes – and with much more kindness; you feel altogether more hopeful for no apparent reason and your interests and attitudes change and move in subtle ways hard to describe.

You cannot articulate exactly what is different – only that most of the time you feel more content with a greater sense of self-worth, meaning and depth. Always there is this background feeling of wholeness and greater depth, making you more sensitive to the impact of outer things. Probably, this is why you are more inclined to discard activities you used to enjoy, but which now strike you as superficial.

The fact that you have embarked upon a vibrant, new way of living becomes increasingly obvious to you. You cannot help but notice how this process of self-inquiry is enabling you to find a living connection with the roots of your being, bringing a natural ability to discern the essence of outer situations more easily too.

There is greater clarity all round as things in your life fall into place, and you feel more grounded and stable. It is a promising sign that you are on the right track.

Then as you try to live consciously from this new standpoint, you will find that each new day offers a creative opportunity to begin anew; the reverberations of one's basic intentions – felt most clearly upon awakening from sleep – will continue to resonate and permeate all your waking hours.

A profound process of transformation is now undoubtedly under way – and this process in its own good time and manner – will take you beyond yourself to your original state of freedom.

The heartfelt longing for truth may be disguised or just faintly felt to begin with, but it does increase in urgency and sometimes takes the form of a summons – an unspoken invitation to lead a better and more noble life. It is when we respond to this summons whole-heartedly that the path to the source of reality opens out before us and at last becomes clearly visible to our inward gaze.

7

Being Is One

The simple dictum of the ancient philosophy of life often described as the Perennial Wisdom, because it has for so long stood the test of time, can be summed up in just a few terse words: 'Thou art That'.

We can say it easily enough, but still fail to fully appreciate the depth of meaning contained in such a cryptic saying – or any other phrases pointing to the same truth, for that matter. 'Being is One' – and basically everyone is That. This is the essential teaching to be found running through the heart of all the great world religions.

Yes, we are all different sparks of the same fire, and this simple analogy at the very beginning of the spiritual quest is enough. It is almost all we need to know – yet we will probably still need a lifetime to put into practice this profound fact that we are not actually separate from the whole of reality – although we behave as if we are. It is mankind's stubborn sense of separation from the totality of life that is the cause of immense conflict and unnecessary suffering.

For my part – during almost my entire life it seems – I have been closely engaged in an intense search for exactly this kind of interior knowledge. Nothing else would do as far as I was concerned; the quest for unity of vision has always been my central and fervent aspiration.

And it has always been striking for me to see how this insistent, existential inquiry is without end, clarifying one's doubts and allaying one's fears as they arise without ceasing, in response to the continual challenges of daily living.

For an increasing number of spiritual seekers in the West, the crucial question 'Who am I?', as a direct means of contacting essential being, has become their preferred approach to bring harmony and resolution of difficulties.

* * *

This familiar sense of 'I' – what exactly is it and where does it lead when it is followed through to its hidden origin within us? This pivotal thought is unique and not like all the other thoughts, that are dependent upon it. The word 'I' refers immediately to the centrality of one's existence – it is the primary concept upon which all other ideas are based, like pearls strung on a necklace.

Just to say 'I' straightens us up and connects us to the roots of our being, where we feel stable and strong. Above all, we are certain that we exist and can declare unequivocally. 'I am that I am'.

This ancient approach of Self-inquiry belongs to the Indian tradition of non-dual wisdom, showing a tried and tested way to true knowledge of the deeper Self within every human being. This direct path is regarded as being of inestimable value by devotees of Vedanta, but it is not the only one by any means, for there are as many methods to approach truth as there are in existence different people.

It is important to realise that key fact, if we are not to fall prey to narrow-minded intolerance and become a burden to all around us as a result. Leaving aside our own preferences, we can rest assured that whenever in all sincerity – someone, somewhere – calls out to the supreme power, in any way at all, there is *always* an answer. And furthermore, one can be certain that the response from the universe is always totally appropriate to the needs of the moment – such is the assurance that simple faith offers.

When we ardently look to God, for example, the answer to our prayers apparently comes from on high – from outside and above us. But when we direct our attention inside, it is from deep within one's own mind that the response seems to emerge – and the necessary strength is given in the manner best suited to us. The point is that it is our sincerity and willingness to trust in a higher power that counts – not the method.

* * *

Spiritual practice does not require the mastery of a huge mass of theory – just an unflinching curiosity and a certain, existential grasp of what is true in your own experience, together with a determination to stand by your deepest convictions.

It is fashionable to repeat nowadays that 'small is beautiful', and indeed in a spiritual sense, as well as in small-scale economics for which the phrase was originally coined as a book title by Fritz Schumacher back in 1973, it is quite true that a beautiful simplicity may offer the best way forward. In the spiritual life, a firm faith often comes from the smallest and most unpromising of beginnings – and it is a marvel how such a transformation in someone's outlook can occur against all the odds.

In biblical tradition, it is also claimed in the most bracing of analogies drawn from Nature that 'faith can move mountains' – and this sort of age-old, symbolic saying is also emphasising the supreme value of faith, but from the opposite end of the measuring scale.

In spirituality, a certain one-pointed rigour is essential, but still there are no strict rules – the question of faith can be approached in a multitude of different ways. Any subject can be approached from either the positive or negative pole – and Truth may be best found by subtraction, rather by endless addition of theory and speculation.

Absolute Reality is non-objective and cannot adequately be expressed in words as such – and sometimes only by stating what it is not.

Analogies too can only go so far, and the description of

something can never be the same as the described. In just the same way, you can only know what is true for you in the most direct manner – by remaining fully conscious and aware of yourself as you are in all simplicity. At such a time, you are merging with the deeper ground of being – and you are no longer apart from it, as you are gently drawn into stillness.

To stay still, to be constant in purpose, to contemplate steadily and in quietude what you already are in essence – this is what meditation is all about. Accordingly, the easiest way to become naturally aware of this primary truth that one is not separate from the whole of life is to simply remain quiet – and allow the underlying truth of things to reveal itself.

An approach like this may seem simple enough, but it is by no means always easy, because moment by moment it requires the willingness for us to face up to our actual state of mind – rather than how we would prefer to be, and according to how we would like to be viewed by others too. Straight and narrow is the path leading to eternal life, as the Bible says, but now perhaps we may catch an inkling of what this really means.

Radical acceptance of the way we truly are – not in theory but on the level of raw humanity – takes guts and tenacity and requires our all. Inner work of this kind is progressive and thorough and is not done in a day, as our inner nature is churned and purified of its defilements.

While straddling two worlds – the outer scene of practical living and the subtle, shifting landscape of inward experience – we are obliged to walk on the razor's edge. To learn to do just that, constitutes the fierce challenge of our unfolding journey.

8

The Only Revolution

The teachings set out here are by no means strict articles of faith, but they *are* intended to be put to the test in daily life in the most natural way possible – and revised according to experience.

You could even say there are no definite teachings as such – just wise advice pointing in a helpful direction. This is because all genuine spiritual insights leading to deeper understanding flow finally from nowhere else but from our own being initially and then beyond that – from the very source of existence.

In other words, we intuitively know these truths already – even if they still need to be made conscious for us, before they can be recognised and put into practice. In authentic spirituality – whatever great religion it has emerged from – there are certainly some essential guidelines, as well as sound, practical methods to introduce direct experience of truths described, but there can be no cut and dried rules.

Dogma and rigid concepts tend to confuse us and block any sense of an unforced freedom. Coercion under any disguise sounds the death knell to the natural unfolding into spiritual maturity. The crucial point is that, having done our best to absorb the instructions offered to us – and having done so at our own pace to enable us to clearly formulate them in our unique way – we are free to continue upon the path we have freely chosen.

We then need to step aside for this wider and deeper consciousness to make its presence felt within us. This is what could be called 'taking the long view', because it is a creative process of natural transformation that cannot be hurried.

The signs of progress may be all about us, but well hidden in the mundane details of our daily life, where the use of intelligence and basic common sense remain indispensable to help us discern what is the sometimes, subtle difference between genuine truth and cleverly disguised falsehood.

Yet an important turning point occurs when we realise that – far beyond theory, technique and discussion – our actual life *is* the spiritual practice. There is no real sense of separation any more between the so-called teachings and us; they have both become part and parcel of our way of being.

At heart, although physical distinctions remain, we know by now that, at the deepest level, we belong to the universe – and are one with it by our very nature. In a mystical sense, we are always united with the divine, which can never be apart from us, because that would be an impossibility by virtue of Oneness.

This view of the sacred represents a complete reversal in our outlook. It is perhaps the only genuine and worthwhile revolution – and it is likely to have long-term consequences of the most far-reaching kind. From now on, in discomfort as well as in ease, the richness of life to some degree is always seen to be here – so there is no longer the pressing need to look elsewhere. This is the moment when the penny drops – and we finally get the point.

Throughout our entire life, we have simply been working with the raw material of suffering and joy – hope and fear – moulding it into the unique pattern most suitable for us, and then assimilating the lessons we have needed to learn. Seen like that, nothing at all – no matter how difficult or dreadful it has seemed – has been wasted experience to be discarded. It has all been grist for the mill – and what a great relief it is to know that.

This is a significant moment for us and we should take care not to pass over it too lightly or swiftly – for life unfolds moment by moment according to the quality of our awareness. The degree of clarity depends upon the ability to observe mind and body as an undivided unit – as already complete in wholeness.

We must be willing to learn anew at every step in this new and more mindful manner. We must try to remain vigilant and unfurnished – open to all possibilities. It is a gracious art of living, which takes care to leave nothing out as all that appears to us is made welcome in our receptive consciousness.

* * *

We can observe how so-called ordinary daily life looks quite different in the light of this radically fresh perspective. Our most fundamental sense of faith has now become rooted, less in a system of belief and more in the reality of our own existence. It has become somehow fused with the greater Reality, which underlies everything. This profound turn-about in our perception is sometimes spoken of in spiritual terms as a metanoia – a total reorientation of attitude and vision. Whatever its significance, it is a wonderful opportunity to begin again from scratch.

Such a radical shift is not a direct result of our doing and you could regard it as a gift of Grace, but it must be true also that our previous efforts cannot have gone in vain. This is because all those attempts to break through the barrier of our limitations must have contributed to the critical moment of awakening to that sacred, universal ground of consciousness, in which we have always lived, moved and had our being.

On the level of the individual in terms of character-building, there is still always room for improvement and here one can obviously speak of making progress in moral rectitude. But in a spiritual sense, we cannot really talk about progress.

This once again is because in truth, we are already perfect in our essential nature of purity – intimately related to the Absolute for all eternity. It is a paradox, because on the relative level of passing time, that is nonsensical of course – and we would be foolish to claim to onlookers that our ultimate perfection has any immediate bearing upon normal daily life.

Yet indirectly it still does – if only because the realm of time is upheld by the eternal background, without which it cannot exist.

Gradually these points become clear to us as our discernment grows, but it is always important not to confuse levels of being and functioning if common sense distinctions are to be given their rightful place.

In conclusion to this chapter, it is worth mentioning that the pattern of our interior life naturally falls into cycles of development according to individual circumstances; periods of ease alternate with periods of difficulty; there are times when we feel as if we are moving forward in clarity and other moments when we simply get stuck. It is all quite usual within the overall perspective of the path.

Sometimes it seems as if our very life resembles a varied landscape of plains, valleys and rolling hills. One grand vista succeeds another, inviting our exploration as the horizon recedes – but we never seem to arrive anywhere.

At the beginning of the spiritual quest, multiple questions are asked of the teacher in one's initial zeal and they are disposed of patiently one by one if he or she is skilful – even as many conflicts are resolved, provided the spiritual instructions we have been receiving have been sound. But there comes a time when, no matter how good our teachers have been, our troubles seem to return ten-fold – invigorated as if they had never gone away. Then we may wonder where we have gone wrong.

The mysterious fact is that spiritual development ascends in a spiral and problems recur higher up the spiral than they were before – but nothing is wrong with that. Vigilance needs to attend our further efforts – that is all – as we persevere, while continuing to move onwards and upwards towards the goal. Eventually, if we are tenacious, we are bound to find the unobstructed vision we are seeking, in which the totality of our life can be viewed in all its beauty and immediacy.

9

This Place Called Here

In this vital inner work upon ourselves – so often misunderstood and misrepresented as simplistic or impractical – we are attempting to return to the very roots of our existence, the ground of our being.

But far from being irresponsible, it is in real terms a courageous and worthy thing to do – no matter how it may be viewed by a sceptical world, which is more accustomed to outer achievements, yielding tangible benefits, than to inward reflection with no obvious or immediate, practical application.

Spiritual practice of the contemplative kind considered here may be regarded as a variation and extension of psychotherapy – a skilful means of training the mind and heart to fully relate to the challenges of everyday living in a more courageous and creative way. It is perhaps in this ethical and religious sphere – and on the causal level – that authentic spirituality's true worth resides.

Insofar as it possible to formulate one's intention in words, we are in effect seeking to fashion anew the substance of our personal consciousness. It would be a daunting task if it were our responsibility alone, but fortunately it is not – since inward growth is a natural process, while still of course remaining dependent on goodwill and perseverance on our part.

The work of cleansing and stabilising the mind needs to be thorough, and it will only proceed at a natural pace without being forced. Even so, it will not be long before we spot a difference in our habitual responses to the irksome, inconvenience of daily life – that is, if we persist in our spiritual studies.

Bit by bit, we are informed by deeper understanding and increasingly upheld by our growing trust in a Higher Power that created us in the first place – although how or why It has done so will always remain a great mystery.

Yet that is the real point. It is precisely this not-knowing, regarding our existential predicament that keeps us open to truth's hushed and often inscrutable impartations. These precious insights arise when they will – according to our precise need – but they seem always to flow from within our own consciousness, whatever that may turn out to be.

Before long, our findings present us with a radical choice. Is consciousness a mere product of the brain's functioning, as conventional science would assert, or is conscious awareness evidence of a dynamic energy with an autonomy of its own and originating from another realm altogether?

* * *

This much is certain – that the location of the personal sense of identity called 'I', which is so familiar to us, is what we commonly refer to as 'here'. It is precisely in this indefinable place, where without fail we can always find the absolute conviction that we exist.

This mind of ours is a quietly aware natural space, inward in the first instance but also extending to our outer environment. It feels all-encompassing, without boundaries and although we cannot say exactly what it is, we feel naturally at home there.

So, within us resides all possibilities – our entire potential for good or ill already exists in this unfathomable store of qualities, which constitutes the mind. We may seem to have the power of choice, but our predispositions often win the day to determine the eventual outcome of events – and it is the way in which we regard what happens to us that turns out to be crucial.

If we have basic goodwill, the necessary guidance regarding the best way to proceed upon the path of life seems to be always forthcoming from the universe – although from the outset, we have no way of knowing in quite what form those hints will appear.

We should lay down no conditions, but we should constantly remain alert to discern the next step along the way. Our life is precious and the attitude we adopt towards its varying aspects will make or mar our fortunes and determine the extent of our suffering or happiness.

Our viewpoint provides the key to what will happen next, and success will hinge on a simple change of outlook as we become less self-centred. To our surprise, we find we no longer rely entirely on our own efforts, as we see the futility in always having done that.

So, the constant and tiresome question: 'How can I do it?' – can become instead a more tranquil and utterly heartfelt pledge to surrender our vain efforts for the sake of Truth. But in the final resort, we may still have no other choice but turn to prayer and make this plea, born out of sheer desperation:

'You act in me for once. I can do no more – you sustain me in all my ways.'

Such an ardent request to God comes to us spontaneously, born out of genuine need. Yet when the call is sincere, the response from the universal power is equally unmistakeable too in the sense of joy and relief it brings.

When in this manner we are wholehearted in our approach to our difficulties, we feel the strength of a quiet dignity enfolding and uplifting us. This noble quality that enables us bravely to stand firm in the face of adversity is beautiful and liberating in its spacious and generous outreach.

We can see then just how important it is to be always willing to learn anew, while being prepared to move forward in unaccustomed ways – sometimes well outside our comfort zone.

10

Roads to Reality

It is ironic isn't it? All roads lead to reality in a spiritual sense, because there is nowhere else to go, and yet most of us still need to traverse an area of rough terrain that seems obligatory in the quest for Truth.

If you look for a logical explanation, you can soon find one. A capacity for spirituality, expressed poignantly through heartfelt devotion, is inherent within most human beings, but not everyone is aware of their own hidden promise of greatness and so cannot fulfil their true potential.

Although the quality of deep devotion is always present, it often remains quiescent, possibly because it has not yet been touched by the power of love. Ultimately, it is only the gentle touch of love that can awaken anyone's devotion to God – nothing else can replace love.

It is sobering to consider that love alone – and nothing other than this most profound of emotions – can fully take us beyond our own apparent limitations and grant us a more expansive viewpoint. But it is a reassuring thought also, because it allows us to trust that everything in our experience will be taken care of, once we determine to rely on this deeper power.

It is often said that Love will 'always find a way', yet it is helpful to remember too that there is no such thing as 'one approach fits all' when it comes to spirituality. By that very token, it is evident that not everyone is inclined by temperament to a devotional path.

Just as well then that there are plenty of alternative approaches, with a gradient suited to every need. Nobody need ever feel they are left out in the cold, as far as spiritual practice is concerned. Not only that – we are always homeward bound, even when we appear to be heading in the wrong direction. Such is God's mercy that we are never beyond His reach.

* * *

The reader can hardly have failed to notice already that an unconventional blend of spiritual influences pervades the chapters so far. Brought up and baptised as an Anglican, the writer takes a broadly ecumenical approach to Christianity, but it is an unusual stance – and one touched by mysticism too.

It is a unique viewpoint that has been further transformed by a prolonged exposure to Hindu and Buddhist teachings about non-duality. And this expression 'non-duality' is an explanatory term, which may be unfamiliar to some people, but is frequently used these days to express the clear understanding that there is only oneness – 'one without a second'.

Any written work is bound to be crafted in the light of the influences brought to bear upon its author. This book emphasises moderation in all things on the level of our basic humanity, but it goes further in matters of faith to espouse a universal approach. As such it is a book with the potential to bridge the divide between sharply opposing religious views – while embracing the aspiration to close the gulf between sacred and secular standpoints. In the light of non-duality, differences of opinion exist of course, but there is no real separation between opposing positions – and no justification for outright confrontation.

It is a tall order, but possibly only such an all-embracing, holistic approach to the intractable problems of the world can find consensus and introduce a much-needed spirit of cooperation into international affairs. It is only this spirit of loving kindness and non-violence that has the quiet but profound power, fully capable of ushering in an era of greater peace during times of the greatest anxiety.

It is surely far better to emphasise what different religions have in common than to focus upon whatever divisive elements keep them apart. It makes good sense to remain flexible and open to varying opinions; this is liberating for us, as it opens our eyes to parallel truths in different religions, encouraging tolerance, while aiding the dissolution of age-old conflicts.

In the light of this integrated understanding, one sees with renewed clarity how Christian devotions are not fundamentally different from the practices of prayer and adoration in Hinduism, Islam – or in any of the other great religious traditions for that matter. The Perennial Philosophy honours the Truth wherever it is to be found; its adherents down the ages have always recognised differences of approach, while honouring the veracity of their essence.

* * *

The Indian devotional way is known as Bhakti Yoga – the word 'yoga' denoting 'union' and the word 'bhakti' meaning 'fondness for homage'. It is a dualistic approach, gradual in its nurturing of aspiration and a spirit of dedication to the Supreme, and it stands in marked contrast to Jnana Yoga – or the way of knowledge, which is more direct and immediate in the precious insights it yields.

This direct way in Hindu spirituality is sometimes called 'the short path' in contrast to the 'long path' of more gradual purification. And it is in accordance with this radical approach of Self-inquiry, that one is instructed to look inwards and immediately try to uncover the root of the I-sense – the source of consciousness within oneself, where our higher Self ever abides.

Not infrequently though, this bare and direct mode of approach to our inner life can seem just too dry and austere. And certainly, this kind of existential quest for insight can run into the sand whenever negative emotions are too strong – and run riot. Our mind is far too agitated for meditation at such times.

It is then that we may have no other option but to ease off and turn to less intensive ways for a while. To devote oneself in service to family, friends and neighbours – with undivided attention, but away from our own affairs – may help somewhat to reduce the self-concern that can be so painful and isolating. This would be to engage in Karma Yoga – the path of good works.

Yet in classical Hinduism, there is one more option available for the aspiring seeker – and that is Raja Yoga, the royal path of self-mastery. Such may be the path most suitable for those resolute souls, who prefer a framework of firm discipline to support their efforts. For them, nothing can surpass this noble but somewhat stern way of spiritual accomplishment.

To reflect deeply upon what you are in the clear light of reality, is undoubtedly the most natural yet profound form of meditation there is. Once mastered, it is a practice that you can return to as often as you like - and it always brings peace and reassurance, provided it is the right approach for you. I can vouch for that.

But finally, when all is said and done – and especially in our hours of greatest need – to simply pray to God in all sincerity and devotion is probably the quickest and easiest way for most people to return to the ground of their being in order to recover a sense of balanced perspective.

In those critical moments, we are reaching out into the spiritual sky of Heaven like an innocent child – and this we should never be ashamed to do, just because it may appear to us to be childish or a sign of weakness. There is nothing weak about devotion; it is in fact a sign of genuine aspiration that grows in us as we cultivate the soil of consciousness.

As we begin to work on ourselves inwardly, in whatever way comes most naturally, we will see how necessary it is for us to weed out with resolute patience all that impedes our progress. It may be hard going at times, but there is no alternative if we really want to find lasting satisfaction in life.

Never mind the difficulties. It is in this diligent way that we are preparing the foundations of a stable place within our internal awareness where we may settle and call home. And it is from this inward refuge – this place called here – that we can draw the necessary strength to meet the outer world with its interminable problems and demands.

11

Awakening to Immensity

Once you determine to take the plunge in any new phase of life, quite often everything seems to fall beautifully into place, as if it was meant to be. There is a sense of something slotting-in – the beginning of a resolution in what had seemed so complicated and muddled before.

Nothing obliges you to behave in a radically different way, so it is something of a marvel when you plainly see for yourself the need to accept everything for the best now, just as it comes – and without so much protest.

And every time you remember to put first things first and simply attend to the roots of conscious awareness within yourself, you notice with renewed relief how all the rest seems to more easily follow on.

When once you begin to find the true origin of yourself there at the source of thought – and sense the mystery of really being at the centre of your own existence – you will find too that you are no longer knocked off balance so much by outward events. Less affected by outer impacts, you will find it easier to remain relatively calm under pressure and stress. It is a considerable step forward.

Acceptance of everything that transpires in our experience is not mere passivity – it is a positive attitude by which you make the best of what you cannot avoid. Acceptance cannot possibly be a panacea for all ills, but it brings into difficult and disharmonious situations an element of graciousness, which tends to function as a healing balm, resolving conflict and attuning us to the natural rhythm of the universe.

When this happens, difficulties may remain, but there is no longer the added problem of your resistance to them, which causes extra and unnecessary suffering.

That clear light of seeing set deep within the mind – that impassive, and watchful element within us that is the witness – can stop us in our tracks when necessary and enables us to pause our constant, headlong rush from one task to another without due consideration.

It is not always easy to admit that our continual activity may be a compensation for an unwillingness to face the uneasy way we feel. When we do recognise the uncomfortable truth of that sense of insecurity, however, we can refrain from following every single impulse. It is a distinct relief to begin to slow down and become more diligent in our approach to everyday duties.

As we become accustomed to it, the decision to simply stay with the stillness within us, is found to be quietly restorative. It is a great thing to find a safe refuge and leave aside for a time those intractable, troubles of the world. We find that the fundamental awareness of our own existence is utterly normal – and to remain tranquil, steady and sane is to get to know well the wonderful sense of peace that begins to permeate our consciousness in any quiet moments.

As insights begin to dawn from deep within, we feel finally unencumbered and set free to be more ourselves. Harmonious action can then naturally proceed from clear seeing, and in straightforward terms, this just means we will intuitively know better what to do – as well as when to begin. We can plainly see what is appropriate in any given situation.

* * *

The most direct and natural truth is simple and permits no digression in its firmness. The past no longer exists as such and the future has not yet come – so the living moment is the only moment that really matters.

And whether remaining still or active physically, our basic

attitude should remain constant. It is best to make as little distinction as possible between inner and outer experience, knowing in principle at least that both aspects are opposite ends of the complete picture – the spontaneous wholeness of living that cannot be arbitrarily divided.

The central focus of attention is always in the immediacy of the present moment. Whenever we sit quietly in meditation, for example, we begin to note whatever is the totality of our experience – without judgement or choice, but simply by allowing feelings, thoughts and bodily sensations to be exactly as they are – without trying to manipulate them in any way.

This is what is known in Buddhist circles as mindfulness – the methodical practice of paying close attention to our subjective experience just as we find it – moment by moment and whether we are standing, sitting, walking or lying down.

These are the four postures, as traditionally stated in Buddhist scriptures, that cover all outward human activities. And since internal awareness knows no boundaries, the discipline of mindfulness can be applied equally to the business of living, wherever we are and whatever we are doing; it is an approach that works just as effectively in activity as it does during times of repose.

Our entire life in fact can be embraced by this attitude of alert attention – mindfulness can become for us a mainstay of our daily routine and a reliable internal support to our endeavours in good times and bad. Mindfulness is truly a spiritual practice for all seasons. When we determine to take it up, we are commencing a liberating process of self-discovery that progressively releases hidden tensions in mind and body.

It resolves emotional knots, just by making us aware of those blocks before allowing them to dissolve and fade away in the light of our kindly observation. To sum up - it can be said for sure that the regular practice of mindful attention to the most ordinary of activities, has the penetrating power to transform the quality of our experience.

Quietly following our breathing as we meditate in the manner described, is an effective means to help us stay focussed. To quietly follow the breath is to bring mind and body together and as we let go of all efforts to control the mind during our periods of sitting, we will see how any turbulence will gradually settle to allow a natural feeling of ease and harmony to emerge instead.

Then when we return to normal activity after such a period of repose, we will notice how natural it is to continue in that same alert state, which notices everything that occurs moment by moment. Quite simply we awaken to the vastness of the world as we look out at it – and to our astonishment, we find we do not feel any more separate from the immediacy of our outward experience than we did when we stayed still in the quiet refuge of meditation.

Furthermore, we will notice how dynamic action arises out of this immediacy – as and when necessary. How we stand is quite the reverse from what we have always assumed. The universe is now expressing itself *through* us – it is living our life, breathing our breath moment by moment.

Even as we continue to do whatever we need to do, according to our free will and circumstances, we recognise that it is not really us doing it – ultimately, we are being lived by the indwelling life that sustains us.

This radical change of perspective – from a dualistic and fragmented perception to global seeing – is something of a revelation. Nevertheless, it is a way of looking that is so simple and obvious once you have noticed it, that it is all too easy to overlook its significance.

The importance of this insight is that the world appears *within* us – and not the other way around. We stand there – not merely as insignificant creatures forever separate from all we behold – but instead as containers of the vast and beautiful scene in all its intricate and spectacular glory.

You could say that we have become formless in our own right – empty of a separate self and transparent to the truth of things. We realise now, not only that we exist, but that we exist far beyond the outlines of our individual form – and are not limited by its attributes.

By understanding just how natural this perception of the totality is, we are set free to enjoy the abundance of the universe aright. This simple but hidden truth is what the great mystics of the world have always known and celebrated.

12

True Abundance Revealed

Spiritual insights arise naturally, but the sincerity of our intentions paves the way. It is always when we manage to put our doubts aside and relate with the totality of our own consciousness to life in its entirety, that we come spontaneously back into right relationship with the whole world.

As suggested in the last chapter, our personal experience is a matter of direct and immediate perception. When we remain fully present to life moment by moment, we become open to receive the immensity of the universe within the embrace of our own being. The radical simplicity of this alternative way of seeing strikes us with renewed surprise each time we notice it, but we cannot ignore its plain and persuasive truth.

There is no doubt about it whatsoever. In terms of our immediate sensing – whether through the organs of sight, hearing or touch – we can find no strict dividing line, standing between us as a person and the world we see as outside. These two distinct aspects of living – interior and exterior – are actually one and the same, completing a seamless whole. This is the startling revelation that the direct approach of non-duality offers.

This immediate perception of the truth of how things are in each instant – according to our subjective experience – radically alters the quality of our life. The clear recognition that consciousness underlies everything and penetrates everything – that it is omnipresent, omniscient and omnipotent – changes our world-view utterly.

When we realise that – as far as our essence is concerned – we are not apart from the people and things that surround us, many conflicts resolve and difficulties in relationship ease. We feel a natural empathy with others; we more easily sense our shared humanity and a natural kindness and compassion arises within us. These are the welcome fruits of any genuine spiritual practice – but they are consequences that are particularly evident in the alternative approach to perception that underpins this study of the direct path to Self-knowledge.

* * *

The idea of universal faith follows on naturally from this viewpoint that sees all created life as whole – diverse but undivided. The very notion of such a natural faith, free of the constraints of dogma and released from age-old prejudices that inevitably stem from ignorance and greed, is surely a liberating one.

But to be realistic, it could only become a transformative possibility for humanity if a far greater number of people felt able to leave their fixed and narrow views behind and see the world in a more broadly holistic manner than they do at present.

It always seems surprising, and a great pity, that the majority of the population do not already think that way, since to regard all living creatures with respect would seem normal enough to any right-thinking person. Courtesy is certainly a prerequisite for compassion. Only such a fundamentally humane attitude is worthy of our full humanity – irrespective of whether we see things in sacred or secular terms.

As we continue to contemplate these universal truths, we begin to see how the single light of consciousness pervading all existence, naturally brings forth the rich abundance of the earth. This natural fecundity finds expression in an overflowing prodigality, but much of this abundant wealth gets wasted so long as it is viewed in a materialistic manner – and strictly in terms of supply.

For it is with the crucial division of the spoils that the tragedy of injustice begins to unfold. It is always the same story. The fruits of the earth tend to be shared out in unfair measure by those in power – in favour of the rich, while neglecting the poor, who continue to languish.

Materialism is at the root of injustice, because true abundance is a natural attribute of consciousness – the unforced expression of generosity – and not just a matter of physical supply. Simple abundance is a natural expression of Life itself, which ever seeks to sustain everything – if It is only allowed to do so.

Since it is intrinsic to life, abundance is never lacking – even in the state of undeniable poverty, which could be tackled more effectively with a fairer economic system. But when a full yield of a vital harvest is interrupted by war or natural disaster, for example, the true nature of supply is inevitably obscured – and the harsh struggle for survival commences. This is when the gulf between rich and poor widens further and is of course how terrible famines take hold.

Disasters at least serve a grim purpose if they serve to remind us just how precious life is. When we learn to value life fully – then we may realise anew just how generous Nature always would be in its prodigality.

We should remember this cardinal truth: that there could be a sufficiency for everyone in this beautiful world, if only natural abundance was never squandered out of hand or its rich availability abused for selfish reasons.

13

Open to the Unknown

We tend to assume far too much about what an individual's life truly *is* – in other words what it really signifies for us to be alive at all – let alone where its deeper significance may lie as far as ultimate reality is concerned.

Our central problem in this difficult day and age seems to be one of identity. Lacking the most lively and rebellious sort of curiosity, many people seem to fight shy of straying far beyond the established norms of selfhood. Perhaps they do not question deeply enough who they are in spiritual terms, and so do not dare to venture their all in a quest to unearth the possible origin of their human identity.

If we care to probe more deeply into the profound question of what it really means to be a human being, this fascinating mystery of the simple fact of our existence soon gives rise to further reflections.

Granted that we are undoubtedly alive now by some miracle, what is the very best that can be accomplished with the rare privilege of having been conceived and safely born in the first place? It is another important question surely worth asking.

Whatever value you ascribe to the undoubted truth of your own existence, it is clearly a wonderful thing to have been granted the precious boon of human birth. I would suggest then that the prospect of being allowed to live – even for one more day – by the gracious dispensation of our mysterious Creator, is not an opportunity to be wasted if you can possibly avoid doing so.

So how often do you make time to seriously consider these intriguing questions, which offer such profound food for thought in our ongoing endeavour to make sense of the tedious daily round – and find deep purpose in living?

And if you do ever reflect along these lines, does it not sometimes strike you just how difficult it is to seize the day, hour or even single moment of your fleeting experience long enough to carefully study it?

Time in fact often seems to take delight in teasing us, as it slips out of sight and just out of reach – yet again. Do we not find it so? The unavoidable actuality is that time is always moving on with inexorable precision, and we cannot hold it fast – no matter how hard we try. On these occasions, we find we are contending with Time itself in its most furtive guise as stern teacher of the most unyielding truths of the universe – joy and suffering, impermanence and death.

Such abrupt encounters with the evanescent nature of time – so often yielding pain and sadness – can seem to test us almost beyond endurance. Yet moments like these can also prove to be supremely valuable opportunities, because they insist that we return to the central core of our existence, which is timeless – and partakes of eternity's peace beyond earthly measurement.

At the very centre of the turning wheel of the world is utter stillness – and only when we lose touch with the central truth of our conscious awareness through confusion and forgetfulness, do we tend to lose our way in outer darkness. That is why it is so good to remain mindful of our thoughts and actions as best we can. As soon as we notice we have drifted away, we simply return to the centre point – and begin again.

When we cannot help but resist the unceasing flow of time – as we struggle with its unsparing demands – we are often aghast to see how unyielding our multiple attachments are. It is then that we glimpse the futility of holding on to situations, which can so easily turn from pleasure to pain.

Caught up in turmoil, it is always tempting to reach out for tidy formulas, by which we hope to cope with stress in a more secure and orderly manner. But by reducing our horizons to familiar limits, we risk denying ourselves fresh chances to grow in maturity, as we master new skills.

If on the other hand, we drop our assumptions about how events should turn out, we may come to sense the boundless delight of not-quite-knowing *what* will happen next. It is amazing, for example, to see harmony emerging out of discord when we least expect it, or to notice how the most intractable of difficulties resolve easily as if they never existed.

Much of our resistance comes simply from a most understandable wish to avoid suffering, but often situations we have dreaded turn out to be nothing like as unpleasant as we imagined they would be.

If we are willing to 'sit loose to life' without expectations, we enter effortlessly into a deeper rhythm, which is in harmony with the underlying laws of the universe. This universal principle of harmony will become for us a cloak of protection so long as we try to live in accordance with its directions.

When we finally give up our efforts to control what happens to us – when at last we are prepared to meet life head-on without always taking refuge in preconceived ideas – we become open to the unknown.

It is then that we come under the merciful dispensation of Love, which always acts in freedom. Love is always searching for new ways to embrace us in forgiveness for those acts of omission and commission, which we prefer to forget – and which left to ourselves we would most certainly never forgive. That is the unforgettable mercy of love, which will never betray us.

14

The Steadiness of Being

Make no mistake about it – there is no such thing as a mistake in the ultimate sense. This is because even apparent mistakes are allowed in the wholeness of life that includes everything. The darkness and the light, the rough and the smooth, what is easy and what is unbearably difficult – all these facets of experience further spiritual growth when regarded in a positive light.

It is undeniably true that the steadiness of an authentic spirituality expresses itself primarily in the grounded optimism of moderation. Consistency, reliability, a quiet trust in the universal principles of harmony; all these wholesome qualities provide a firm foundation for an orderly life.

Nevertheless, a mature spiritual outlook cannot afford to be unrealistic about human nature and must remember to make allowances for the shocking extremes of human conduct. Never a day passes without further examples surfacing in the news of appalling behaviour that nevertheless should not always be rejected out of hand – but embraced instead with compassionate understanding.

Figures in public life are expected nowadays to be of exemplary character as a matter of course, but we all have feet of clay under certain circumstances. Notwithstanding lapses of judgement, the willingness to admit mistakes or show remorse following wrong-doing, is always a good indication of a person's essential decency. Nobody is altogether beyond forgiveness, but redemption requires the abandonment of pride and malevolent intentions.

From the spiritual point of view, a background sense of order in someone's life may well be suggestive of genuine virtue, which arises spontaneously from recognition of the sacred nature of life. Unfortunately, however, signs of simple goodness are all too frequently misconstrued in these secular times as rather a dull indication of mere respectability, which in turn may be regarded as old-fashioned or mediocre. In truth it is nothing of the sort.

A typical person of a modern mind-set – in preference to the steadiness afforded by a meditative lifestyle – usually craves the stimulation provided by the continual challenges of contemporary living. Exciting new developments frequently hold out the beguiling prospect of endless progress, but all too often utterly fail to deliver enduring fulfilment.

Cynicism and a general lack of trust in traditional values, spring from oft-repeated disappointment and the unceasing demands of commercialisation, which leave little time for sober reflection upon the true significance of human life.

* * *

Turning aside decisively from superficial distractions, it is good to ascribe the highest importance to spiritual practice – yet there is a careful balance to be struck. When we become too intense concerning our spiritual pursuits, or alternatively push too hard against the natural tide of events, we run the risk of focussing upon our spiritual progress at the expense of our ordinary affairs.

After all – in the final analysis – it is obvious that being is far more important than interminable doing. In other words, people are far more important than things, while even having a great deal of possessions, or achieving more and more success, pales after a while. Our 'things' include all those pet notions of ours, which tempt us at times to brush all else aside in pursuit of our goals – but in disregard of common sense.

This may tend to happen whenever we are overtaken by self-centred enthusiasm for whatever spiritual path we have been drawn to follow, and which we may by then be inclined to foist upon others. How wearisome all that becomes, once one has seen through such an inclination – understandable as it is.

The secret hope to convert others to our point of view is bound to cause conflict in our personal relationships sooner or later. It may also encourage a subtle form of egoism, which is hard for us to detect, because it is so difficult to remain objective concerning one's own failings. It is only natural to seek for genuine freedom of spirit – to reach out in all sincerity to make meaningful contact with the true inner light – but it is imperative we do not seek to transcend our natural humanity in the process.

Our immediate task is to remain where we find ourselves in the present moment – for this is where our duty lies and where fresh opportunities to make progress will become naturally available to us.

If we fulfil the demands of this present moment with goodwill, we can be sure that the future will take care of itself, but if we neglect our immediate obligations, we will only succeed in storing up yet more problems for the future – all of them needing to be resolved with even greater difficulty later.

* * *

In its own good time, the gentle but penetrating practice of mindfulness will shed valuable light on all the neglected corners of our existence, cleansing and renewing us as it does so.

From the beginning, what is of the most crucial importance is our integrity, since we will stand or fall according to the quality of our intention. It cannot be said too often that we do not live in isolation. One's personal consciousness is not merely one's own private domain – it is simultaneously the *True Consciousness*, which informs all living beings and so is universal in nature.

Since Life abides in unity – there can be no secondary or lesser consciousness. In the turmoil of daily life, we can forget this basic fact all too easily, but to recall it is the *Real Remembrance*. Each time we bring this basic truth to mind, we feel somehow held by It. We become aware of a deep sense of belonging to the totality of existence – without even caring to know what that supreme reality really is.

The ability to articulate the insights one has received is not necessary either. More significant is the fact that when you realise that you are somehow part of everything – and not really separate from anyone else except in strictly personal terms – you will know finally what solidarity means.

Wherever you happen to be – whether in the thick of things or on the side-lines – you will experience an uplifting sense of unity and can no longer feel isolated or lonely. At last you can emphatically declare that you belong to humanity – and take delight in that. In Buddhist terms, such empathy is what is known as 'sympathetic joy'.

From now on, you will be participating in the positive experiences of other people – but by the same token, you cannot avoid shouldering their burden of sorrow either. That too, is a privilege – yet you do not mind at all. By then, you have come to feel that showing compassion is the very least you can do as a responsible human being – at last dedicated to bringing harmony and reconciliation to a disordered world.

15

By a New and Living Way

To proceed *by a new and living way* is to make a fresh resolve to live according to the principles of truth as we are now beginning to understand them.

This gradual appreciation of what we have been gleaning about spiritual life, needs to be thoroughly woven into the very fabric of our being, to transform over time, the way we respond to the daily challenges we face on all levels of our experience.

Authentic faith is neither blind nor idealistic, for it is linked indissolubly to a higher principle now activated in our consciousness. Meaningful change can only occur with the introduction of this higher element, which penetrates in its potency any uplifting ideas we have already received that stem from truth.

We will now need to try and live by the light of any such inspiring thoughts that have deeply struck us. Then we will have made these pointers truly our own and they will sustain us unfailingly as we traverse any rough terrain on the spiritual journey still to come.

Words that flow from Truth remind us of its beauty – and take us swiftly back to the source of wisdom within ourselves. It is only there in the conscious source of life where we find our true being, that our persistent doubts and painful regrets can ever find final resolution.

The past – by the very definition of that word – is always well and truly over by the time we recall it, but that of course does not mean that we have nothing left to learn in the present moment from what has gone before.

We have all made mistakes and have done or said things we bitterly regret, and those thoughts and actions have left traces in mind and body. Such residues have a powerful momentum and continue to influence our behaviour in sometimes incomprehensible ways. Our past behaviour patterns need to become more clearly apparent to us, if the process of healing is to properly commence.

Having absorbed spiritual instructions and taken them to heart, we can bring to bear upon the pains of the past this higher healing principle that comes from deep awareness of the inner laws that govern spiritual awakening. In this way, residues from past errors gradually dissolve and we are set free from our age-old burdens, as inner wounds begin to heal.

We may have passed through many rites of passage along the way and these hard times need to emerge from memory into the light of our conscious awareness, as we reflect deeply upon the complex factors that have shaped our past life.

The task of understanding and eliminating past physical and emotional trauma is an important stage of spiritual practice we should not evade – and need not fear. Nevertheless, it does need to be attended to with resolute courage and a quiet dignity – and the necessary strength to accomplish it will always be forthcoming if we trust that this will indeed be so.

Conflict resolution will enable us to untangle knots in relationships that have brought forth great pain, and although this can often be an arduous process, it is one that yields peace, together with the hope that this difficult work will prove possible for us – notwithstanding our prior misgiving.

* * *

How glibly summed up, but how difficult to accomplish in our own social sphere, let alone on the ground in the wider world where age-old conflicts spill painfully out into the open for all to see. Conflict resolution is a fundamental life-skill, which needs to develop from our earliest years in everyday situations with parents, family and friends.

We learn best through experience as we go along – initially

at home during childhood of course, before being encouraged to relate constructively with all those we meet, as we move out into society – through school and from thence into the workplace.

To act as a go-between in intractable situations, when there is a stand-off between opposing parties, is a difficult task which is everyone's responsibility to attempt in adult life. Repeated failures remind us like nothing else can that the process of resolving conflict must always start with non-violence.

The capacity to restore harmony all around us, will always depend upon an attitude of basic goodwill on our part – directed towards oneself in the first instance. At the heart of conflict resolution, lies an attitude of flexibility; a yielding and compassionate nature is essential, together with patience to persist in situations of deadlock and the willingness to forgive others when love has failed. One cannot pretend that it is easy – only that if we persevere, love will always win the day in the long run.

Before we can hope to help others, however, we will need to embark upon a vital journey of self-healing – with no idea of how much distance we must cover, or how long the process of cure will take. But to start with, it is always a good idea to turn to our personal beginnings for elucidation, as we comb our earliest recollections for clues as to why things turned out quite the way they did.

Our early memories are particularly valuable, because they hold the key to a deeper understanding of the true purpose of life. This early period of our development was a time – more crucial than any other – when the positive seeds of faith, courage and intuitive perception were originally sown in the field of our consciousness.

As we become aware of these seeds, we cultivate them with our close attention and bring forth in the present moment the very qualities that will most likely serve as hard rations to nourish us further down the road.

Part Two

A Transforming Fire

16

How the Heart Grows Wise

It must be nearly 60 years ago now, but I can recall the scene almost as if it were yesterday. I remember the very particular texture and smell of the leather boxing gloves, as well as the taut feel of the ropes behind my back and the definite thrill of stepping into the ring before the big fight.

And what a fight that last one was for me. As a boy of ten at boarding school, I was facing an opponent far tougher than I was. For the first few rounds, I staunchly held my ground and threw some hard punches as good as I got. But then the tough, young fighter opposing me landed a well-aimed blow to my nose – and it began to bleed profusely.

I had to endure further heavy punishment from him, while I left a long trail of blood behind me around the ring as I stubbornly refused to give up the fight. Finally, the referee called time on this uneven bout, to the sympathetic applause of the ringside onlookers. But there was a satisfying twist to the tale as far as I was concerned. I may have lost this key, junior match decisively, but I was awarded 'Best Loser's Cup' at the prizegiving in compensation for my bravery.

Understandably then, I could not help but feel that perhaps I was the true victor, as I basked in the warm glow of my own courage as well as in the genuine admiration of the watching crowd.

* * *

On the face of it, the scene I have just described is merely an insignificant memory from my own boyhood, but in hindsight I regard it as noteworthy, because it was a formative experience and provides a definite hint of the very distinct path through life I was to follow.

At numerous points along the way, the road would seem particularly hard, and it was then that the spirit of tenacious fortitude would prove indispensable. It cannot be a coincidence that the courageous resilience I spontaneously displayed on that occasion long ago would be the resolute quality I have always most admired in others – and held up as a guiding light. It is through hardship that the heart grows wise.

Development and refinement of a child's deeper propensities may equally well be accomplished by distinctly physical challenges, or by taxing, emotional situations resulting in considerable stress. It all depends on the innate character of the young individual. But what is undeniable is that the heart gathers inward strength and wisdom through adversity.

An inclination towards spirituality is a gift like any other, but it does appear to be predetermined, revealing itself in a child's loyal and affectionate nature, marked out by candour and a disinclination to entertain falsehood.

The marked presence in a young person of fine qualities like courage are an indication of a warm heart, already beginning to awaken to its potential for nobility – as well as suggesting the likelihood that, later on in life, the child will find it possible to offer unconditional love to others, while being receptive to beauty in its countless forms.

These attractive characteristics can undoubtedly be further nurtured through a balanced system of education. Yet it is equally true that every young person without exception – and whatever their cultural background – carries the possibility deep within themselves to awaken to an awareness of spirituality. This is so, even if early signs of spiritual development are lacking and the quality of education being offered falls short of ideal.

Nobody is beyond reach of help and whenever deep interest in Truth arises in anyone's heart and mind, all manner of positive qualities will follow naturally in its wake, so that a life of creative fulfilment is assured – even though that individual may be sorely tested by adverse circumstances.

On the interior journey to authentic life, the mind needs to be informed by clarity, so that the intelligence of natural discernment is awakened, regarding what truly matters. But, in the final analysis, our onward growth into spiritual maturity is all about education of the heart – because if the warm quality of affection is lacking, life will always remain fundamentally sterile and empty of deeper meaning.

The nature of our start in life – the manner through which inherited traits and external influences have acted upon our innate gifts and inclinations – will doubtless determine the initial direction we will take.

But the uneven path onwards must be taken alone – and the way we respond to the vicissitudes we meet is crucial. Early on in life, the quiet and invisible voice of conscience – our inherent moral sense – is not yet ready to fulfil its critical task as interior spiritual guide.

Yet as we mature, under the pressure of testing experiences, in due course the clear flame of the awakened heart will shine brightly enough to enable us to traverse the most arduous of internal landscapes without either losing our way – or being overwhelmed by despondency.

17

A Crime that Did Not Pay

The invisible light of conscience lies deeper than any thought-construct, but nevertheless shines through the medium of mind and emotions, in the potent influence it yields.

The quiet voice of conscience comes directly from the soul – the essence of being, which comprises our very heart of hearts. And this heartfelt warmth lying just below the surface of every child's awareness indicates the presence of natural goodness – an innocence, crying out for protection, yet so often denied.

That being so, the primary challenge of a sound and balanced education should of course be to ensure that this vulnerability is not exploited – that a young person's innate moral sense is neither side-lined by academic requirements, nor obscured by the competitive pressures of growing-up.

In the present day, unfortunately, while reports of childhood abuse are widespread, those ideal educational requirements are certainly not always met. Aware of that, I feel fortunate that I did receive in the 1950s and 1960s a good all-round education. It was a solid, traditional sort of beginning, which somehow still had this nurturing aspect. And that was the case, even though my boarding school was of the institutional, character-building variety.

Its pupils in my time were lucky to have a particularly easy-going Headmaster – a kindly man, who had endured harrowing, front-line service in the muddy trenches of the First World War. Most understandably, he was reluctant to impose on his charges a stern or punitive regime, but his broad-minded approach to education in that generally disciplined era, set him apart from his colleagues, while the boys gained unquestioning benefit from his markedly genial manner.

The result was that the atmosphere of this private school in a pleasant, forested area of England close to the south coast, offered its pupils ample space and freedom for youthful exploration. I was at ease in that creative community setting and can see clearly now how conditions there were especially conducive for the development of integrity and reflectiveness in an already sensitive boy.

It was in this beneficial environment and at this somewhat special preparatory school, that for the very first time my own conscience felt free to declare its own truth clearly – and with the silent voice of undeniable authority.

* * *

At school – as in life – peer pressure counts for a great deal. I discovered this to my cost when one summer term I was persuaded to join a gang of other boys as they roamed the extensive playing fields in their spare time, looking for something absorbing to claim their restless curiosity.

And I suppose it was inevitable that before too long, the even tenor of my studies would be interrupted, as I unwisely became drawn into the gang's ambitious plan to build a hut in the grounds from any odd bits and pieces of wood they could find.

Nails and tools essential for a sound job all needed to be found from somewhere of course, and so the ringleaders hatched a plan to sneak out of our dormitory at dead of night to fetch what was required from the home of one of the gang members, whose parents lived nearby.

It soon became evident that the brave volunteer needed a good disguise before he set out in the dark. Undeterred by such an obstacle, one of the boys soon located just the right clothing in the school janitor's store-room – or so he thought.

Being rather too easily influenced and anxious to please, that was the critical moment when I became an accessory to the plot.

I was enlisted to fetch the clothes from the janitor's room right away – and instructed to leave the bundle in the half-completed hut to be used as needed.

As surprising as it may seem, it never occurred to me that what I was being asked to do was wrong. If I thought about it at all, I must have considered that to simply 'borrow' someone else's clothing for a while was harmless enough – and I could return the missing articles soon enough without being found out.

However, my conscience begged to differ in no uncertain terms, and the instant I entered the janitor's room to remove his jacket from its hook, I was filled with a sense of deep unease, made much worse when the contents of the capacious pockets tumbled to the ground.

Brushing my severe misgivings aside, I furtively gathered up the fallen things and hastily quit the scene with the misappropriated jacket. But I was in deep trouble – and I did not have to wait long to feel the dire repercussions of my ill-considered actions.

Our form teacher was grim-faced when we gathered in class the next morning. The master reported that there had been a mysterious theft of clothing from the janitor's store-room, but luckily the missing items had already been spotted on the floor of a hut in the grounds by a passing member of staff.

Our teacher said he did not believe for a moment that any of us could possibly have anything to do with this most unfortunate incident, but he had to ask us – just in case we could shed any light on the mystery.

I have never been much good at withholding the truth, and I immediately held up my hand to admit this curious crime. The master was taken aback by that immediate confession by a member of his own class. Somehow, however, although my misdemeanour was considered serious, I escaped with just a minor punishment – and this must have been thanks to the fact that I had done the decent thing and owned up immediately.

The headmaster's leniency did not prevent him from firmly lecturing the entire school some weeks later, about the woeful collapse of discipline, which had occurred that term. It was at the annual prizegiving ceremony – held as usual in front of all the parents – that he spoke out so forcefully.

It was totally unlike this kindly man to talk as sternly as he did, but as far as I was concerned, there was no doubt about the implications. I was obviously one of the main targets of his wrath – and I have never felt more mortified than I did that afternoon.

The sense of shame was overwhelming by the time I joined my elder brother and parents in their car after that awkward assembly had dispersed. My brother had told them all about my misdemeanour – and I was greeted in the car by their stony silence of disapproval.

I felt miserable right enough, but at least I had discovered the plain truth that crime never pays. It was a salutary lesson that I have never forgotten – and now I know something else of extra value too:

I will always be able to rely on my own conscience to shed unfailing light on the perplexities of living, whenever the going gets tough. And, furthermore, it is good to know that there is always something positive to be retrieved from the most unfortunate of situations.

* * *

Amidst the perilous uncertainty of these troubled times, how innocent that heedless prank from long ago now seems – especially in comparison with the hardships that children in reduced circumstances are often forced to endure nowadays.

The minor tribulations I underwent during a sheltered upbringing are as nothing compared with the suffering presently being experienced by lots of young people, afflicted by appalling conditions of poverty and conflict in the most deprived parts of the world.

And yet that insignificant incident in the relatively tranquil conditions of post-war Britain, still represented a distinct rite of passage for the small boy I was then – and its importance in the wider scheme of things cannot be entirely discounted.

When it comes to tracing the delicate outlines of human development, the most valuable clues to our character often reside in the smallest of details – and we overlook them at our peril.

18

Blessings in Disguise

To adopt the courageous standpoint that adversity may turn out to be a blessing in disguise is an enlightened approach to one's troubles, which is always likely to stand us in good stead.

This is radical optimism, to say the least – foolhardy perhaps, but not entirely misplaced. It is just a useful way to proceed with the assumption that the glass from which we must drink for sustenance is at least half full – and not perpetually half empty to confirm a dispirited frame of mind.

While that is hardly the smartest of analogies, it is at least homely and goes straight to the point. To emphasise the positive whenever possible does us the greatest of favours and need not be regarded as unrealistic.

It is true that to view a spell of severe misfortune as anything else but a hard blow of fate, does require a degree of fortitude that, although admirable, may be a step too far for most people.

Yet the willingness, notwithstanding adversity, to persist in the brave attempt to place unhappy events in a wider perspective soon brings its own reward. This can come quickly in a welcome release from bitterness and a sense of freedom from a nagging regret that things did not unfold as they should – and could have been altogether better, if only circumstances had been different from how they transpired.

Not all upsets or mistakes carry equal weight of course. Many accidents have trivial consequences, while others may be of cardinal significance, because of their far-reaching effects. In the same manner, some decisions reveal themselves to be crucial, vested with the apparent power to determine our very destiny. These choices we cannot help but regard as critical, because they seem to have been predestined somehow – simply by virtue of the way they have slotted so easily into our life-pattern.

* * *

In the light of such conclusions, it is sobering for me to consider how the course of my own life was irretrievably defined by a single, dramatic road accident involving my parents.

I was just 17 years old and in my final year at public school during term-time, when they both drove off in search of a new house deep in the countryside – far away from the affluent area near London where our family had lived for many years.

They had evidently agreed to make a fresh start in a desperate bid to rescue their seriously troubled marriage, but their house-hunting trip was to end abruptly in disaster. How unfair that seems, and yet the reasons for such a grave outcome will always remain cloaked in mystery – beyond our ken, like so many of life's unexpected twists and turns.

On this inauspicious day of sunshine and heavy showers in early summer, the straight and narrow road they were travelling on was soaked and slippery after rain. A powerful car coming at speed in the opposite direction, attempted to overtake a line of three lorries, but skidded in the wet before slamming into my parents' vehicle head-on.

Nobody was killed in the severe impact of the crash, but my parents' high-performance sports car was written off and they were both badly injured in the collision. In those days before seat-belts, my mother struck the windscreen and suffered heavy bleeding from multiple cuts, while my father, who had been driving, broke a leg and punctured a lung.

They took months to recover from their injuries. A kind nurse was to sit by my mother's bedside, holding her hand through that first night in hospital as she struggled to survive. It was touch and go, but she pulled through the crisis on that occasion by dint of her fierce will to live. The courageous battle for life took her final reserves of strength nevertheless – and just three years later she died from cancer, quite possibly brought on by the long-term shock of this catastrophic accident.

My mother was just 54 years old and had potentially many years of active life before her. What happened to my parents seems an utterly pointless tragedy – and yet unless that terrible motor accident had occurred, I could never have been granted the invaluable freedom at such an early age to travel widely in quest of Truth.

That much is certain – and so, in a certain way, one could suggest that my mother had sacrificed her life for the benefit of myself and my brother, who has shared my deep interest in spiritual matters. It is ironic how things turn out – and how deeper meaning and beauty can still be found, even in the sadness of catastrophe.

It is a grave reminder that selfless acts on the part of those who have cared for us to the best of their ability, are no small matter and should never be taken for granted. That would be a careless betrayal of love, which is always as sad as it is unforgivable.

* * *

Out of the blue, I had received a fleeting premonition of the accident just a few days before it happened. That previous weekend, my parents had attended our school Speech Day celebrations and I recall how we all had enjoyed a festive picnic alongside our gleaming car, parked together with many others on the spacious playing fields.

Later that afternoon, the proud parents joined all the boys as they gathered for Assembly, held outside in the main school yard. The place was reached by steps and I looked on as my mother ascended them, looking especially attractive in her smart, black suit.

Her smiling face, framed by an elegant hat worn for this

special occasion, was lit up in the bright sunlight while she paused for a moment before joining everyone in the yard. In that single instant, I was somehow struck and held fast. It was as if time stood still as I was touched deeply by the image of rare beauty that the very sight of my mother had evoked within me that moment – for no reason I could understand.

That precious beauty I had glimpsed was not limited to this world of transitory appearances but seemed to dwell instead far beyond what I was witnessing – in an imperishable realm where the joy of love and the sorrow of loss abide for all eternity. Words cannot possibly do justice to this poignant awareness of deep sadness that came and went in an instant.

It would be just a day or so later that I was summoned to the Housemaster's study to be told of the fateful accident – and then it was as if a shadow had fallen across the sunlight of my expectations. As I waited to leave school at the end of that term, I was not only on the threshold of adulthood, but drastic changes were now imminent in what had been up to that point a sheltered life. Things at home could never be quite the same again.

19

The Tipping Point

Life often appears to be utterly unsparing in its demands, but sometimes it does seem that hard knocks are needed to incline someone towards a life of greater faith, or more complete integrity.

Who can possibly say what might be required in any situation, to bring about this marked shift in a person's attitude – a real change of heart? But often it is sudden trauma that tips the balance to bring about a vital change of direction and a radically fresh perspective. Losing a valued job, the breakdown of a cherished relationship, or the immense sadness of sudden bereavement – all of these are surely good enough reasons for depression, if not despair.

No facile explanation can ever satisfy an anguished demand for a proper answer to life's unbearable dilemmas, but sometimes one knows from one's own experience, that a stringent remedy in the form of a crisis, may be the only thing that will bring someone to their senses – if they have been pursuing what is clearly a mistaken or deeply damaging path for them or society.

Upheavals or reverses in fortune in life are never punishments as such, but they can represent a tough teaching, because it is never easy to witness the demolition of one's resistance to the ongoing flow of events, which happen not to be to our liking.

I have previously written extensively about the healing power of pain, and I remain thoroughly convinced of the veracity of this approach that suggests that we often learn more effectively through difficulty than through ease.

The tipping point in my own life occurred without warning in early adulthood, when a promising career in the caring professions was abruptly cut short by a psychiatric breakdown.

I became seriously disturbed after a love affair with a fellow student had broken up in the middle of our nurse training.

I was exceptionally vulnerable at that point – and some understandable reasons were not far to find. I had been devastated by the premature death of my mother from cancer eight years earlier when I had just come of age; in addition – in common with many of my contemporaries in the 1960s – heedless sampling of psychedelic drugs around that time had left me susceptible to psychological problems.

And there was one more factor that had considerable bearing on my over-sensitive state of mind. I had recently returned from extensive travels in India where I had gone in quest of Truth. I had been exposed to rough living conditions and my physical health had been compromised; it would have been an unsettling time of transition for anyone.

I soon recovered from this initial breakdown, but I remained subject to periodic bouts of psychiatric instability for many years to come – although I was fine in between and continued to work normally in my new profession as an antiquarian bookseller.

I am thoroughly convinced that the psychiatric disturbances to which I had apparently become so liable, were closely connected with my intense, spiritual seeking, which was putting my sensitive nervous system under intolerable strain. Conventional medical opinion remains far from accepting such an alternative view of so-called mental illness, but the weight of evidence supports this far more compassionate approach to mental and emotional turmoil.

A counsel of perfection is always out of place, but it is obvious that without being completely honest with oneself, it is hardly possible to approach absolute integrity – through which one becomes completely straightforward and can appear fully trustworthy in the eyes of others too.

If you look closely enough, you will always get an immediate sense of whatever may have seriously gone amiss in your affairs.

To retain a realistic awareness of one's deficiencies – to have a wounding knowledge of oneself – is one of the most valuable assets to be kept in reserve for when one is most under pressure.

And this is because, a genuine admission of where one may have gone wrong in one's life, paves the way for profound renewal and makes a process of deep healing possible – despite how terrible things may still appear to be on the surface.

The most significant turning point for me personally, was the time I fully accepted what for me at that stage in my life, was the worst outcome possible – the loss of a career opportunity I had set my heart upon.

The key moment of release came the very second that I said 'yes' to the bitter disappointment I had undergone. It was one of the hardest choices, I had ever had to make. But something magically cleared deep within me then, and I could carry on at peace with whatever came next – no matter what it happened to be.

As later life unfolded, I gradually came to see that a tipping point need not remain confined to examples of personal crisis, but indeed refers to the entire world. A pioneering, contemporary teacher of mindfulness is Jon Kabatt Zinn. He writes most succinctly as follows about this very subject in his excellent book *Coming to Our Senses*:

You don't necessarily have to surrender your life to bear witness to injustice and suffering. The more bearing witness while dwelling in open-hearted awareness becomes a way of life for all of us, the more the world will shift, because the world itself is none other than us. But it is sometimes, more often than not, a long slow process, the work of generations. And yet, at times, a tipping point is reached that could not be predicted even one moment before. And then things shift, rotate, transform – and very quickly.

20

A World behind Walls

Some impressions are so deeply etched in memory that they never fade. And there is frequently a resonant quality to retained images such as these, which later tend to serve as significant reference points upon our interior journey on the path of living. That observation certainly holds good, regarding my own recollections of several, memorable weeks, when I helped care for a group of patients with mental health issues in a long-stay psychiatric ward. Whenever I bring to my mind those spells on duty at the vast, grey Scottish hospital where I underwent training as a psychiatric nurse, what is immediately uppermost for me is the strong sense of confinement I experienced.

The large, bare ward always seemed gloomy and dark on those winter days in the Highlands long ago. The male patients either sat around the room on benches – listless and depressed – or they paced up and down anxiously like trapped animals in a cage.

In the meantime, members of staff came and went through the main door – to be kept locked at all other times. As we looked to the men's basic needs during our shift, we were their appointed keepers – and our time on duty with little to do for hours on end, hung heavily on our hands as our own boredom grew. Our patients meanwhile just moved around uneasily – and they had little to do except to wait for the next meal, which was everything for them.

Our charges seemed for the most part forsaken souls. Morose or withdrawn; speaking in riddles, or mumbling gibberish as they frequently did, meaningful communication with them seemed an impossibility – and yet the spark of life within them glowed still, flickering up now and then in surprising moments of clarity or humour.

Caring for them could have been a dour and unrewarding task to say the least, and yet curiously I felt privileged to be entrusted with an unusual job like that, which seemed to belong to a bygone age of grim institutions or workhouses for the destitute from altogether another century.

I was a keen young man from a privileged background, who had never known lack. But nevertheless, somehow there I was – a caretaker for sorry inmates in a sombre space where the sun hardly ever shone. The windows loomed large in that old hospital building, but it hardly mattered what size they were, for they overlooked an outer scene, which had faded from memory forever for those long-term patients with virtually no prospect of release.

It was a forsaken place for sure, but in hindsight I can see there was cogent reasons for having been drawn to this kind of caring work. My eldest brother had suffered severe, physical trauma during his difficult birth – and he grew up with cognitive disabilities. He was unable to cope with normal schooling and, before long, required permanent institutional care in a psychiatric hospital, much the same as the one where I was presently training. Having grown up alongside a close relative with mental health issues, it was hardly surprising I had developed a natural affinity for unfortunate people in a similar plight to my own brother.

I often wondered accordingly how one could bring a quality of joy into the lives of these forgotten men in Scotland. The trouble was – the inactivity and lack of light in their ward soon weighed me down, so that before long a feeling of weary impotence came up – even after one had only been shut in with the patients for a short while. Looking after them properly was evidently far more demanding than one might think at first sight.

My clear wish to invoke the Light in this most inhospitable of settings was admirable enough and – bearing in mind my family background too – suggested I had a clear vocation to care for the unfortunate and dispossessed. But what I did not fully realise then, was that the wish to descend into this pit of darkness also brought with it an obligation to encounter the forces of disorder and instability within myself.

And the task I was so eager to accept in my inexperience would prove to be by no means a momentary one either – but a lifelong commitment to unearth deeply hidden inner truths. From an esoteric perspective, it represented nothing less than the profound alchemy of inward transformation by which one seeks to turn the dross of ignorance into the shining gold of illumination.

Glowing language like that was most certainly out-of-place in a psychiatric hospital 40 years ago, yet even so, the profound facts of psychoanalysis cannot be denied so easily. In symbolic terms, you could say that the time had now come for me to plunge into the deep and murky waters of the unconscious mind – whether I liked it or not.

This would prove to be that decisive moment when the ordered routine of my days crumbled without warning – and my life fell apart. It was the critical moment when an unwelcome vulnerability from the past caught up with me in no uncertain terms.

At such a significant juncture in my chosen career, it was a crisis that I could have done well without. But in the end, it turned out to be an important rite of passage – and something unpleasant that I no longer need to sweep under the carpet. It is a hard truth, but a salutary one nonetheless – we do not always realise what is best for us in the long run. Ironically it is the most unfortunate events in life that often prove to be the most valuable – and by far the best means of bringing this stern message home to us.

21

Keys to Freedom

You will never know what freedom really is until it is abruptly taken away with a peremptory disregard for your own views on that vital subject. It is one thing to experience the chafing restrictions of confinement from an outside perspective as a detached observer – it is quite another to encounter imprisonment from the inside of restrictive walls, as – without ceremony – you are robbed of the normal freedom to move around without let or hindrance.

That is precisely what I discovered, however, when as a male nurse in Scotland, an unexpected crisis interrupted my plans, while training for a meaningful career in the caring professions. The painful impact of losing through unforeseen, psychiatric breakdown an opportunity for work that I had long cherished, would continue to reverberate in a feeling of disappointment for years as it irreversibly shaped the course of my life thereafter.

One moment I was a respected member of a nursing team caring for patients in the long-stay ward of a psychiatric hospital, and almost the next point in time, I found myself a luckless patient, locked up along with other sufferers in an acute psychiatric ward – and being looked after by nurses, some of whom were also my fellow students. It was a devastating situation – and brought a sobering realisation of just how much had been lost when freedom had suddenly been denied me.

* * *

It was not the first time I had been admitted to hospital due to psychiatric disturbance, and unhappily it would not be the last either, as I continued to be plagued periodically by psychotic symptoms, which had first surfaced to blow my mind away, after taking psychedelic drugs.

In the years that followed, one crisis succeeded another with an almost monotonous regularity to unsettle the ordered routine of family life – and the initiating factor prior to these brief episodes of psychiatric disturbance was virtually always one and the same.

It was my insistent participation in various kinds of spiritual practice – either at home or on intensive retreats with other spiritual seekers – that would often precipitate flashbacks to those symptoms of acute anxiety and high energy, which were originally produced under the influence of drugs such as marijuana and LSD.

At such times, I would totally lose touch with ordinary reality as my awareness expanded beyond the normal boundaries, which delineate our conventional sense of a separate identity. Initially, the experience would usually be one of great bliss and elation, but afterwards all sorts of delusions could arise to cause confusion and dysfunctional behaviour. I believed I was enlightened, but the world around me did not agree – and with hindsight I can certainly understand why.

It always seemed sadly ironic that sincere and wholesome interests such as prayer and meditation, which were intended to deliver harmony and peace-of-mind, should instead be the means of my undoing as far as practical daily life was concerned. But at least it was encouraging to see how quickly I usually recovered from these unstable episodes to resume my normal responsibilities. It suggested that I had no serious personality disorder – and this chimed with my own convictions.

Well-meaning offers of help from friends and family, in the meantime, were never in short supply but mostly it would be of no avail. Even some well-respected spiritual teachers, whom I consulted during this troubled time, could only help to some extent with guidance and moral support.

Increasingly I began to realise that no amount of positive input from outside sources would prove effective so long as penetrating insight into the root causes of my problem eluded me. In the end, the course of action to be taken would have to remain up to me – I would have to instigate my own healing; I could not expect anyone else to do what only I could accomplish.

Understandably, my hard-pressed wife felt overwhelmed by the continual uncertainty surrounding my periodic instability. At least, conventional medicine with its reliance on the blunt instrument of restraint through medication, was always there as a last resort. But the doctors I saw could offer her little more support than I was being given. They had little time for my spiritual protestations and were distinctly puzzled by my relapses – not to mention my strange pattern of symptoms, which did not fit readily into an established diagnosis.

Impatient as they were with my relapses, it soon became all too evident that they had absolutely no constructive suggestions to make, regarding a lasting cure. We were on our own as far as my long-term stability was concerned, and for my wife's sake – as well as for my own – I needed to take full responsibility for our next steps on the road to recovery.

* * *

Mental health issues are still viewed with considerable unease by society at large, but thankfully they no longer carry the crushing stigma that they undoubtedly did when I was young. It is amazing to see in fact what a huge shift has occurred in society's attitude to this painful subject, which was almost totally off-limits years ago, but which is now for the most part viewed with far greater care and compassion – especially too as far more young people are being affected by mental health issues than ever before.

As a sense of crisis over the mental health of the younger

generation mounts, society is at last beginning to acknowledge that the mind and emotions of all individuals are just as important as their body – and we neglect the proper care of all aspects of overall health at our peril.

After all I have gone through with this perplexing issue, it seems utterly clear to me that the true origin of psychiatric disturbance has not yet been fully understood by the medical profession. And this is because conventional medicine is still largely working within a severely limiting paradigm that does not allow for the complete psychic and spiritual structure of a human being to be thoroughly ascertained.

How liberating it is when you permit yourself for once to view psychiatric instability in simple spiritual terms. For example – when you invoke the Light from above, it is only logical that dense darkness from within should arise in fury to obscure your inward vision. And when you turn to Love, you should not be surprised if all that is ignoble and unloving within your unredeemed human nature should clamour selfishly for attention.

Profound inquiry into your sacred origins churns the mind – that is its purpose – but when higher energies touch a mind that is not yet fully grounded, the psyche can easily become unbalanced. In psychotherapeutic terms, this simply means that you should be adequately prepared if you propose to delve into the deep Unconscious.

Any dark sub-conscious material that has been repressed will then tend to surge up from the depths – and if it is does so, you run the risk of being overwhelmed by energies you cannot contain. I am not for a moment suggesting that this radical approach to mental health issues offers an adequate explanation in all instances, but it does go some way to clarify my own predicament.

It may also shed light on the bewildering effects sometimes stemming from the hidden and delicate process of spiritual awakening. Intensive spiritual practice may speed up this process of inner transformation – but it can also complicate it. Full healing of our inward emotional scars proceeds in a subtle manner, which is beyond rational understanding and takes its own time to complete.

* * *

It happened that an essential clue to the possibility of my own cure was present all along. Right in the midst of those troubles – in the face of continuous upheavals – I always felt there was nothing truly wrong with me. I returned to this fundamental conviction regarding my essential wholeness of mind repeatedly – and it gave me the heart to press on.

I regarded the turbulence in my life as a sign of unfinished business – perhaps even from a previous incarnation. Who can say what is the truth of the matter? Irrational and other-worldly as this metaphysical explanation concerning the reality of karma might have seemed to sceptical onlookers, I still clung to it for all my worth.

The difficulties I personally have had to face, have made me more tenacious than ever – and at last I can make full sense of that periodic, psychiatric instability that has dogged my steps. Deep understanding of what factors are involved has finally set me free of such troubles.

Nowadays, I am wary of far-fetched notions and prefer to stick to more measured views. I may have finally found the keys to freedom, but I clearly recognise that a responsible exploration of inward liberty is a lifelong task that leaves no room for complacency.

And what would my advice be for fellow students of Truth who run into similar problems with mental health during their spiritual quest?

Everybody is different – and there are no short cuts or easy answers. You need to remain steadfast with disturbances like that and keep an open mind, responding sensibly to offers of assistance from wherever they come. It may be entirely necessary for you to go down the route of conventional psychiatric care – at least for the time being – but there is nothing shameful in that.

I would suggest that, in the final analysis, perseverance and trust in the unfailing resources of our deeper Self are the most certain keys to unlock the heavy door that bars departure from the dark tunnel of depression. If we never lose hope of finding relief from our troubles, release will certainly come in the end, although not necessarily in the manner we expect.

Eventually, we will be out in the bright sunlight again, but what is most important is that we keep faith while waiting – and with our spiritual convictions intact. We must trust that in the end all will be well. Then we will find that somehow our problems *do* resolve – and we are enabled to claim the repose we deserve. This, at any rate, has been my own experience.

22

Day of Reckoning

As ordinary people, we often seem 'all too human' in our inevitable failings of character and physical vulnerability. But in marked contrast, we simultaneously exist as dignified human beings. Either way, we mirror the universe and as such are richly expressive of diverse, universal qualities – both good and bad.

It is surely by no accident that the incessant dramas of the outer world are reflected in the dramatic events of our own lives, as we are moved by beauty or ensnared by multiple temptations. Every single day – whether we like it or not – each one of us is obliged to witness the inescapable predicament of our shared humanity, with all its contradictions of essential goodness, side by side with the wilful perversity of human nature.

And moment by moment – if we only care to take notice – the continual demands of challenging situations bring to our attention just how precarious and poignant life in the raw really is, when everything is stripped of glitter and superficial appearances.

In recent years, modern living has become increasingly fraught with hidden dangers, but the bare and undeniable fact that physical life can be brutal and short is likely to remain a truism for us, until we are brought up short by an actual emergency.

In some shape or form, the day of reckoning is bound to draw near to everyone at some point. I have no wish to sound an unnecessarily ominous note, but I simply mean to emphasise by this that before death approaches, one will surely be called to account for the way one has lived – and how much one has loved.

We may believe we know this deep truth well enough in

theory, but hard experience has a way of proving just how inadequate mere theoretical knowledge can be. Such moments of crisis tend to occur without warning, most frequently somehow when one is off the beaten track and far from home. It is as if critical situations hold up before our gaze a clear mirror in which we see reflected the inherent fragility of human life – or simply the stark nature of impermanence.

How sadly ironic that one should only realise how fleeting and precious life is, when one sees how easily it can be lost. It was on my recent return journey to India that this sober fact was brought home to me without ceremony – and in no uncertain terms.

* * *

Early one morning in the south of that vast sub-continent, I happened to make a journey by taxi across the beautiful sub-tropical countryside – usually arid but that day verdant in the post-monsoon month of December.

We passed through various small towns and villages on the way, our car threading an uneven path through the tangled mass of pedestrians, animals and traffic in a bedlam of honking and hooting – all quite normal in the general hubbub of Indian life. Out on the open road, our journey seemed even more dangerous than in town, mainly because of my driver's reckless overtaking in the face of oncoming vehicles.

These huge lorries and buses would bear down upon us at breakneck speed and with unpredictable regularity; the fact that we somehow avoided them, seemed far more a matter of good luck than sound judgement.

I was the sole passenger and it seemed as if my driver held my life in his casual hands. I sat on the front seat, hunched forward anxiously, while gazing with tense fascination through the windscreen and earnestly hoping that my own vigilance might help keep us safe.

It soon became apparent that our own good fortune could not be shared with anyone else. On the outskirts of a village we found the progress of our car blocked abruptly by a throng of people in the centre of the road.

Ahead of us on the left, I could see an empty bus lying tilted on its side, but it was the anxious knot of people that immediately drew my attention. We stopped our car and approached the group, after getting out to see what on earth had happened.

The villagers had gathered around a bearded young man, lying awkwardly on his back on the tarmac. There was a huge gash on his head and he seemed rigid in utter stillness. He was quite clearly dead – and some of the onlookers wailed and sobbed as they tried desperately to rouse him. The air was charged with the stark horror of sudden tragedy, but otherwise there was nothing whatever to be done.

The simple country folk seemed understandably dazed by the terrible events of the last few minutes. It would hardly be surprising if this was not the first time some of them had witnessed a needless disaster of this nature, yet their shock at this latest disruption of their daily life was palpable.

By a cruel twist of fate, a precious life had been snatched away with absolutely no warning in a pointless accident, waiting to happen in the chaos of the Indian roads. My driver was told by the villagers that a stray cow had wandered out into the path of a bus and an approaching cyclist had been struck in the ensuing confusion. It was all over in a trice – but for that young man there had been no reprieve from the worst possible outcome.

In the shocked numbness that pervaded the tragic scene – amidst the agonised sorrow of the beseeching relatives – I stood silently for a while, rooted to the spot and totally unable to help, except through the sense of inward calm I felt. Sudden death like that seemed unbelievably harsh and abrupt in that sombre moment, but such tragedies are an unyielding fact of Nature and remind us of the sacred like nothing else can.

It was the very first time I had ever witnessed the immediate aftermath of a crash – and it was a harrowing experience I would not forget in a hurry. I turned away in sadness – and we resumed our journey. We had few words to exchange due to a language barrier, but even if we could have spoken, we were in no mood to talk. This tragic incident had given us both more than a nodding acquaintance with danger – and for me life had suddenly become immensely precious.

23

Dark Face of Reality

Just as authors of fiction naturally tend to draw upon the raw material of their own experience to fashion their characters, so too spiritual writers seek to discern within the circumstances of their lives the most valuable elements of the teachings they live by. Philosophically inclined as they usually are, it is second nature for authors of this meditative turn of mind to distil the essence of wisdom from whatever comes their way – wherever it is to be found.

And there is another aspect of the literary vocation that is a given. It soon becomes plainly evident to any writer – whatever their genre – that you cannot write effectively about what you do not know well at first hand. When it comes to effective communication, only direct experience counts.

* * *

We can extend this analogy to shed light on some important aspects of spiritual practice. It is only in the immediacy of the present moment that the irrepressible vitality of life comes across in the most dynamic way to hit home at the deepest level of our awareness.

Yet if that natural receptivity is barred by emotional knots or some other inner hindrances that we cannot remove on our own – perhaps because we are hardly aware of them – it is obviously going to be difficult for us to make much progress on the path we have chosen.

That much is obvious – but at least it brings me to the main point of these deliberations. There are certain important lessons to be learnt if we want to reach our full spiritual stature. And since at the outset we have little idea of what they are – or how they will be presented – we are in uncharted territory as far as this inward work upon ourselves is concerned.

It is helpful to realise at this point that the testing experiences we require will occur naturally enough in the ordinary course of our affairs. And in this respect, it is also useful to bear in mind that those problems of various kinds which we are bound to face, will all serve one useful end: they will ensure that we remain living in the real world – requiring us to be realistic about meeting the humdrum demands of daily life with practical common sense.

In other words, difficulties are essential, because they keep us humble – and that cannot be other than a good thing. But our resolve to continue following the spiritual path will soon be further tested, because of this necessity of staying down to earth – properly grounded, yet without losing our sensitivity to spiritual things in the process.

That is much easier said than done. We find ourselves living in two distinct worlds – and trying to make sense of two diametrically opposed versions of reality. It can be confusing, to say the least.

* * *

Encompassing two radically different paradigms gets a bit easier when we realise that the problematic realm we occupy is – above all else – an arena of learning. But there too lies the rub. Unfortunately, our ongoing resistance to these vital lessons we need to absorb, is often so considerable that only a truly dreadful event will break through our heedless patterns of living, to bring about a meaningful change of attitude. It is one of the great tragedies of human life that this should so frequently need to be so.

Dire emergencies, threatening life and limb, are happening

all the time of course, but by their unpredictable nature – and most thankfully so – they rarely occur to the majority of people. However, whenever an especially terrible event does happen nowadays, the whole world gets to know about it almost immediately through the global news networks.

We see from this inescapable bombardment of information how everyone is intimately involved in the suffering of everyone else – whether they like it or not. Nobody can fail to notice how much injustice and pain there is in the world, even if they feel helpless to do anything about it.

Here again, it is only living experience that counts and persuades us that we can no longer justify burying our heads in the face of catastrophic global happenings. One of the saddest things about modern life is that we have become almost impervious to bad news. But if you are ever unfortunate enough to have a direct encounter with a really perilous situation – of the kind that we hear about so often – it will doubtless touch you deeply in unforeseen ways too. It is bound to leave an enduring impression in your mind– a memory which will change your attitude completely.

* * *

The tragic accident I had stumbled upon in India without warning, serves to remind me of several other occasions – from the hugely dramatic to the seemingly unimportant – when physical life had suddenly revealed to me its inherent fragility. These were all glimpses of the profound truth of impermanence, but it was only recently that I began to realise how all of them were linked in significance.

As one after another I bring to my mind these diverse situations, I see the implacable expression of a central principle – a fundamental law of Nature, established it would seem, simply to restore the basic harmony of the universe, whenever it falls out of balance.

This restorative principle works unerringly to bring mankind back to its senses, through the suffering experienced when the primary law of love has been disregarded – either in a spirit of malice or just in ignorance. It seems to me highly probable that natural disasters act in much the same manner to restore equilibrium – as if to deliberately counter mankind's insistent abuse of the earth's resources in defiance of basic intelligence.

My earliest memory, signalling a brush with the dark face of reality, finds me as a boy of about nine on a main railway station in London. As I walked across the busy concourse with my mother, I suddenly spotted a man being carried on a stretcher through the gates to a train. His head was shaved bare to the scalp and his face was wan – as pale as can be.

He was evidently grievously ill in a stark way entirely new to me. It was a deeply shocking moment, which came out of the shadows. It was a reminder of the inevitability of death, but of course – with the tender mind of a child – I could not formulate grim conclusions like that.

Around that time, there were other fleeting intimations of mortality – often conveyed by small animals. A pigeon at the end of the garden, strangely paralysed and near to death; a startled rabbit seen on a walk with my father – the animal's face and eyes swollen with the rampant viral disease of myxomatosis.

All these early encounters with suffering, revealing just how precarious life is, were penetrating in quality but bare of overt sensation; only when I was a bit older did the poignant awareness of sadness and grief surge eventually to the fore of my developing mind.

Years later, my wife and I stopped our car to go to the aid of a dog that had just been run over. Its grief-stricken owner was cradling it in the centre of the road – and we saw the animal's tail wagging feebly in final glad recognition of its master, just before it died.

Death's difficult final message speaks insistently of pain and loss – but also of love. It is this poignant legacy of love that always remains in memory to bless us with its delicate fragrance.

24

Guided by Love

By the very nature of our existence, we are above all conscious human beings – and the essence of this consciousness is nothing else but pure love. Not surprisingly then, it is love's delicate beauty – so easily veiled by tribulation – that provides the most telling evidence of the profound consciousness that we really are.

In the bewildering complexity of modern-day life, it is extremely easy to lose sight of something that deep down we already know intuitively, but which we often cannot help but deny. The plain fact is that the real purpose of living is to allow oneself to become a fit channel for the supreme energy of life to flow through us. That current of purity is essentially what love is, in its true nature as a dynamic expression of the Unmanifest.

Yet caught up in the fast-paced round of everyday demands, it seems no small matter for us to admit to a truth so inconceivably bold – so quietly daunting. Somehow the very openness of love often makes us feel uncomfortable, because we are secretly afraid of not being able to live up to its requirements.

Nevertheless, if perhaps we dare commit ourselves unreservedly to love – and finally pledge allegiance to this almighty power that created and sustains us – we may discover to our astonishment how the pure love to which we are drawn so powerfully is never far away. It is always more than ready to forgive our shortcomings, while providing unfailing guidance whenever we most sorely need it.

* * *

Ultimately, love is not something that really needs to be talked about, but a beautiful gift to be valued in our own experience. When once you have been rescued by love, you will know what it is for yourself. And once you have truly loved someone, you will feel its transformative power – nobody needs to tell you about it.

One thing is certain though. After you have been truly touched by the beauty of love, you will no longer be inclined to judge yourself or others so hastily. And by the time the tendency to sit in judgement has seriously begun to decline, a fundamental inclination to harshness will have gone with it, so that you are no longer capable of hating anyone else either.

You will find instead that you have been granted the precious power of forgiveness, so that you are able to let go of past hurts more easily. And there is something else important to note: if you are no longer capable of hating someone, it is because you are no longer angry with yourself for all the wrongs you have done – and for all those other things you have left undone, which have made you a failure in your own eyes.

Thank goodness for that – now you no longer flare up with anger at the slightest provocation, because you see the utter futility of doing so; you clearly see how much pain and destruction anger causes and you have determined to turn your back on it. Also, now you no longer knowingly betray or reject other people, because such behaviour does not belong to the realm of love, to which you have pledged your unswerving loyalty.

But this is the moment hopefully, when the burden of being so good becomes altogether too tedious to carry. Why don't you take another look? Now it comes as a considerable relief to find that you are not exactly perfect – and can be impatient and irritable at times like anyone else. You are certainly no saint – and if you still aspire to sainthood just a bit, it is at least with clear-sighted caution that you do so.

And that is because at long last, you see more clearly that the concept of sainthood, inspiring as it has sometimes been for you, can also become a dangerous myth, easily leading to self-delusion, in the misleading way it can set someone apart from others when it is not appropriate for them. In addition, such delusions of grandeur are states of mind that you yourself have been deceived by often enough, to fail to notice now how easily you can still be enticed by false imaginings.

Time and time again – and on each occasion with grateful surprise – you see how the noble dignity of love prevents it from being abused. Yes – it is always Love itself, fresh and ever new, that reminds us of its incomparable splendour. No wonder, we find ourselves pledged to love and have sought to turn our back on deceit in its myriad of forms.

* * *

The word 'love' is a greatly over-used noun, and we need to utilise it with judicious care, while being clear about what we mean when we refer to its different aspects. It is of course only by relating fully to other people in the cut and thrust of ordinary daily life that we gradually grow in understanding and begin to learn how to love in a mature way.

Many a time, we have endured abrasive encounters with an uncomprehending world, which we have felt in our raw vulnerability to be anything but harmonious or just. And all too often for many of us, relationships in their bewildering variety of texture and range of dynamic intensity, have resembled a refining fire, which seems to exist solely to burn up all that does not properly belong to love.

This cleansing process is uncomfortable to say the least, but when all impediments are stripped away, it is just the essential purity of love that remains in all its sparkling radiance. That true light of love is unmistakeable – and it brings us a great and simple joy to realise that it belongs to our essence, which is inseparable from ultimate reality.

Part Three

Summoned to Serve

25

Kindness Counts Most

They do not have to be grand gestures – small acts of kindness will suffice just as well. A supportive word here, a thoughtful action there, a pleasant smile, a friendly wave in greeting – these are the sort of ordinary but positive contributions that help the world turn around smoothly and can even make the crucial difference between life and death, war and peace.

In the end – after all the fine words and froth of interminable concepts – the most genuine kind of spirituality comes down to those quiet moments when you take the time to really listen to what someone else is saying. It is kindness that counts most on the level of basic human relationships, because genuine kindness is the outcome of an unobtrusive love that is not self-serving.

It is the natural warmth of common decency that paves the way for unselfish love. And more especially, it is the loving concern and decisive action born out of the selfless courage of rescue workers and volunteers that often proves to be the salvation of the world in its hour of greatest need when disaster strikes out of the blue.

There may be no prior knowing of who they might be, or where they have come from, but all those brave helpers, who would never hesitate to offer immediate aid in emergencies, include people of every age and from any walk of life. That list may number those of religious persuasion or none; famous names perhaps, or ordinary folk – totally unaccustomed to the limelight and normally content to live quietly behind the scenes unrecognised.

And all such workers for peace would immediately put any differences aside to join in service to a common cause, sharing a sense of outrage at injustice – together with a determination to uphold at all costs the inviolability of human life. Have not things always been so, during critical times of transition amidst the swirling tides of human affairs?

This noble and thankless task of building an enduring peace amidst the warring factions of the world, begins, not necessarily at the sharp end of conflict, but much nearer home in the ordinary routine of everyday life.

This important work must always be conducted in a spirit of goodwill and consideration for others and what counts most is our basic attitude. Something radically changes within us, with the clear recognition of the small but significant part we have been allocated in the huge drama of the world. It is in the very instant we take responsibility for the state of our own mind and heart, that effective peace-making begins.

* * *

Time and again, one sees the truth of the matter. Before we can effectively engage in the urgent task of outward reconciliation, we first need to begin to make peace with our own inward demons. This happens immediately whenever we manage to touch the central point of purity at the heart of our own being. It is that sparkling purity of love that changes us for the better – and not we ourselves by dint of effort and struggle.

That fundamental purity is innate to all people, but its transformative power cannot fully act, unless the impediments that check its expression are removed. We can accomplish much in this respect through sensible spiritual practice – but not everything. We cannot take the final leap without being aided, no matter how hard we try.

Kindness is one example of a small key that unlocks the door of goodness – and when that door to the eternal beauty springs open, it reveals the hidden river of love that is always flowing for the delight and refreshment of mankind. The river knows the way and does not need to be directed.

Our inherent purity – the very essence of our individual consciousness – belongs to the supreme love that sustains all created life. As human beings, at birth we emerge from the womb of creation, while at death we return to the source of our being. But as long as physical life endures, there is an indwelling healing element within each one of us that is constantly working to bring forth renewed harmony into our experience and to restore the balance of health on every level, whenever it has been disturbed by stress or trauma.

The self-same healing balm is constantly available and works in the world to resolve conflict and deliver peace. It is down to the interwoven nature of all created matter and the operation of natural law that this should be so. Even as the healing process is permitted to continue unobstructed within us while we knowingly cooperate with its beneficent action – just so, the results of increased individual harmony benefit the outer world and aid its uplift.

To work realistically for peace and order on the chaotic periphery of life, is to realise these profound things that underpin any meaningful contribution to the vital task of reconciliation.

26

The Message that Hardship Brings

Truth is impartial and expresses itself through the whole of life and not just in fragments of our choosing. Or to put it another way – allow yourself to fully sense all your outer, physical discomforts as well as uncomfortable feelings within, in order to experience life in its entirety, otherwise your view of the world will be partial and unbalanced because it is incomplete.

Most important of all – always try to hear the message that hardship brings, unwelcome as it often seems. And the reason for this is simple. Paradoxical as it may appear, you are likely to learn far more from difficulty than from ease, which tends to usher in complacency.

This is hard advice to hear, more difficult still to put properly into practice. To expect us to surrender our resistance and self-will completely in a stroke is a tall order. Yet, it becomes increasingly obvious to us that nothing else but a whole-hearted effort to accept the difficulties of life will do, if we are to resolve painful predicaments exacerbated by continuing to argue with reality.

Our habitual non-acceptance of problematic situations would tend to represent an unyielding collision with the facts of the matter. This is not to suggest of course that we are prohibited from introducing necessary changes – only that it is futile to bang our heads against a brick wall, if how we are behaving is equivalent to that.

Perhaps it is fortunate that we will not need to wait long or peer into the far distance to put this demanding philosophy of acceptance to the test – in our own circumstances as well as out in the world at large. Our troubled communities with their endless succession of intractable problems, offer plenty of opportunity for us to begin resolving conflict. Reconciliation through tireless and patient dialogue is what authentic spirituality is truly about.

* * *

It becomes clear that, at critical junctures in international affairs, what is needed above all is the willingness for all parties involved to engage fully with what appear to be impossible situations – but to do so in a more creative and determined manner than ever before.

Quite definitely this is not the time for most people to retreat to the solitary heights of contemplation, but to bring those sublime qualities down into the depths of everyday matters. Mundane affairs must be clarified and uplifted to begin with – for a stable foundation of virtuous living is a prerequisite, not only for an orderly and harmonious personal life, but also for harmony in the workplace and everywhere else. These basic principles are obvious enough, but frequently disregarded – especially in Western societies.

In the East, these truths are more widely recognised and woven into the cultural fabric of society. A simple and fully integrated approach to balanced living is sometimes described in Eastern spiritual tradition as bringing wisdom down from the mountain top and into the market-place. It is a vivid analogy.

Engaged spirituality cannot be effective with adequate preparation of the mind and heart. It is important never to turn aside from the immense sorrow of humanity, but it is equally important not to become overwhelmed by it. The profound efficacy of prayer can only be preserved by a measure of solitude afforded by the conscious withdrawal from worldly affairs at intervals.

We should never downplay the hidden potency of prayer, or the value of personal concern for the state of the world, but there are definite limits as to how much any one individual can accomplish on their own. That being obvious, it is one's attitude to the catalogue of misfortune we witness on a global scale that counts more than direct action. This is because spiritual work is essentially interior in nature and by no means everyone is cut out for the demanding work of an activist.

Intercessory prayer functions first and foremost on the level of cause, which is often regarded as impractical and unavailing by most people, who are accustomed to look only for tangible, outer signs of success or failure. In the final analysis, many people are left with little more than ordinary goodwill. But this can be far more effective than we realise. After all, it still represents the power of compassion – and this in all its rich potential is our greatest asset.

27

Caring from Afar

(Written immediately after news broke of the deadly nerve agent attack in Salisbury.)

Every time the unscrupulous darkness of worldly intrigue, in one of its most chilling forms, impinges upon one's own sensitive awareness, it comes as a fresh shock to the system. It is a stark reminder of just how powerless we all are as individuals, in terms of real influence in the outer scene.

If one cannot even liberate oneself from personal troubles through one's own best efforts, any attempt to drain the swamp of man's persistent iniquity single-handed will certainly fail. The problems of the world are so dire and intractable that even the most well-meaning of collective efforts most often come to nought.

At least it is a healthy sign of an increasing compassion within society when brutal assaults on human dignity elicit at least some outrage from the community at large. But for many of us, an immediate response of sadness, horror or anxiety, is swiftly followed by a familiar sense of despair as we see yet again just how foolish, stubborn and spiteful the worst elements of mankind can be.

I soberly reflect now, as I have so often done before, that the present tyrants of the world were once innocent and helpless small children. But by now, having grown up and totally lost touch with their original innocence, they will mostly have been consigned to perdition by their victims – even while they insist on perpetrating more and more atrocities, utterly scornful of reproach.

Harsh cruelty inflicted upon other human beings seems to mean nothing to dictators – in fact they even seem to delight in it – and so their behaviour remains beyond the pale of human decency, as they inflict with impunity further crimes upon humanity.

The heedless abomination of tyrants is certainly a cause for outrage, but self-righteous fury and condemnation will only take us so far – and can never bring final resolution to bitter enmity and conflict. All too easily we forget that.

If you heap sorrow upon sorrow, you are bound to complicate a crisis, but are unlikely to succeed in detecting or dissolving its origin. In any case, all manner of hatred inevitably begets further hatred to perpetuate an endless cycle of suffering.

There must be a better way to bring about enduring peace – but possibly only true contemplatives can hope to provide an adequate answer to what is obviously an impossible question. In the absence of a tangible answer, at least the few genuine mystics that remain can continue to uphold an anguished world in their fervent prayers.

Yet the central issue remains. What on earth can ordinary people without special influence do to make a difference in the face of the immense problems faced by a world community in crisis? If the most astute statesmen have failed to find a solution, how can the average individual possibly expect to help meet the urgent requirements of sundry, troubled nations – spanning all frontiers, and so often subjected to the flagrant abuse of human rights?

* * *

Here is an extraordinary fact for you to consider – something amazing and true at the deepest level of existence. Whenever you touch the conscious, inward ground of your own awareness, you are also simultaneously in communion with everyone else in the world.

And this is simply because the life-force within us is not

merely of a personal nature but also constitutes a dynamic energy – universal in its all-pervasiveness. The very essence of life is what sustains this collective consciousness, which we all share – even if we are oblivious of its presence. But realisation is power. As soon as we begin to sense the profound truth of our conscious connection with everyone and everything, we begin to experience the beautiful and transformative possibilities flowing from our renewed understanding.

We often feel incapable of helping others, simply because we feel apart from them. Yet an acknowledgement of the reality of this shared consciousness, is enough to open the door to compassion – and this opening to a sense of caring immediately restores a natural empathy.

The underlying truth, supported by cutting-edge science, is that although physical distinctions exist of course, we are not actually separate from one another in an absolute sense. It is this fundamental fact – transposed throughout all levels of perception and experience – that immediately enables us to identify with other people's joys and support them in their sadness.

By the same token, we are implicated in their errors, as well as in their achievements. In like manner, we too are obliged to play our invisible part from afar in doing what we can to bear the immense burden of suffering at the sharp end of conflict – even when we ourselves are not directly involved. When this key insight comes to us, we should take full responsibility for its profound implications – that we are in truth formed by the world and the world is an expression of us.

To reflect deeply about these things is spiritual work of the highest order. It will tend to be undertaken behind the scenes on the causative level, but it is subtle in influence and effect – and we do need to realise that it cannot be assessed in a conventional way. Similarly, the potency of love and prayer cannot be measured in a scientific manner, but even so, a clear awareness of the blessings that prayers yield during times of crisis, carries its own conviction.

Real depth of understanding gives rise to a stalwart faith that cannot be easily subdued by suffering or entirely crushed by conflict and cruelty. Brute force certainly seems to hold sway on the surface of things to begin with, but in the long term, mercy and non-violence will always win out. It is the profound law of love that makes it so.

28

Robe of Many Colours

We live in an age of deceit and complexity when the smallest detail of daily life can cause acute anxiety, often for no other reason than we are already near to being overwhelmed by continual stress – and close to breaking point.

It is a sad reflection on contemporary society that, for countless people in this unstable world, anxiety and fear should now loom so large in their life as a big problem. Yet that being undeniably the case, it would surely be of the utmost assistance for one and all, if only more people could learn to face this kind of fundamental suffering with more insight.

That would at least reduce the dark emotional charge which deep fear contains, by thoroughly understanding the workings of its mechanism. To simply see clearly the movement of fear's painful trajectory within us helps a great deal to lessen its impact.

For anyone following a spiritual path, freedom from fear probably represents the first and last freedom they are seeking. For such practitioners, continuing to face up to fear's assumed menace with tenacity and courage, will quite likely always remain a central plank of their daily practice. But even when the sense of separation from the wholeness of life has faded to a large extent, vestiges of anxiety do remain.

Not only is this quite normal as an unavoidable aspect of physical embodiment, but also our fresh convictions concerning the origins of suffering, take time to become established within the mind. Along the way though, one will have become well used to keeping the basic principles of balance and harmony in mind – and know clearly what still needs to be accomplished by way of facing up to sorrows and difficulties, instead of seeking to evade them.

It is true that most of us have not yet fully staked our claim to the entire territory of our being and are somewhat afraid in consequence, of what may lurk in the unexplored recesses of the mind. In those circumstances, it is understandable too that we may remain somewhat divided and to some degree strangers to ourselves – but at least this gives us a healthy incentive to continue with tenacity on the path we have chosen.

* * *

Although courage manifests in many ways, it is always pleasant to behold and positively uplifting in influence. Fear also appears in multiple guises and is consistent in its effects – but is always acutely unpleasant and casts a shadow over everything. Fear and courage form an inescapable polarity and belong together; you will never discover indomitable courage unless you have first come to know fear well and have done your best to welcome it into your heart.

Fear likes to lurk in corners, troubling us at intervals until it is tackled head-on, while bravery is fearless, standing out boldly for the world to admire. Fortitude is beautiful to see and can be fashioned into robes of many colours – its fine qualities clearly visible as they shine in someone's aura to represent different facets of the radiant nobility of being.

Courage, witnessed through the unselfish acts of others, not only restores our own faith in humanity, but also shields us from suffering too. Whenever examples are brought to our attention of heroism in the face of great danger, or remarkable courage displayed in the sadness of sudden bereavement, it never fails to touch us deeply and puts us in touch once again with the source of our own inner strength.

On the direct path of Self-knowledge, we will certainly need all the courage and tenacity we can muster, but it will not necessarily be of the usual kind people would immediately recognise and admire; it is more likely to be of quite a different order, which can easily be overlooked as nothing much, because it is so deeply hidden.

We must not imagine, however, that inner fortitude is reserved for those of a spiritual disposition. One frequently hears of unsung heroes of all ages – from the very young to the elderly – who have the most difficult issues to contend with and yet still struggle on bravely in impossible situations, while professing no obvious faith at all.

Noticing this, one cannot help but conclude that everyone is on a spiritual path of sorts. We are all striving for betterment as we are sternly put to the test – whether we consciously acknowledge it or not. The process of living includes the necessity of learning from experience. A steep learning curve has nothing to do with any form of belief – nor even whether we ourselves are doing well – or for that matter making an utter mess of our attempts to get on in life as best we can.

* * *

There is nothing strange about stress, aggression or fear; these most normal of human responses belong to the basic survival mechanism of fight and flight, while stemming also from a stark, innate awareness of our inevitable mortality – for everyone is born only to die sooner or later. Yet when our normal fears are made much worse for whatever reason, with additional anxiety leading to panic, the resulting tension can become unbearable – putting a blight upon our entire existence.

Coping with unexpected trauma or a life-threatening diagnosis, are obvious examples of this terrible kind of suffering that people so frequently need to endure. Nobody is spared the prospect of an ordeal of this nature at some point in their life, especially nearing its close.

Yet for someone of faith, there is always the solace of prayer to fall back on. At least then, they can try to pray that somehow a path may be shown through the present darkness – a way found through an ordeal that appears little short of agonising. It may not be at all easy, but if you pray to God like that, and with all the strength at your disposal, the true inner light will most certainly come to you. You will not be left without succour in your hour of greatest need.

In the most critical situations – when we are at our wits' end – it becomes even more urgent for us to attempt to put fear firmly but kindly back in its proper place, in any way we can. Apart from turning to heartfelt prayer, we may do this most effectively by stepping back to observe the movement of acute anxiety within us.

After all we could not become aware of fear at all if we were identical with it. We certainly could not enfold the nagging sense of worry – let alone embrace the most terrible feeling of dread – with loving kindness, if we were not essentially different from it.

Thoughts and feelings constantly come and go in us. Fear is like a particularly unwelcome visitor, but if we simply watch it without getting involved in interminable argument, that most unpleasant of emotions will go on its way after a while – and leave us well alone. The same also holds good for other negative emotions that may hold sway over us.

Society, in accordance with long-held convention, tends to encourage us to think of our individuality as something solid and fixed. But a little meditation quickly shows us that our inner life is always shifting in endless movement – just as the whole of life is caught up in the flux of change. In the fleeting moments that make up our experience of reality, there is nothing permanent about us at all.

The assumption that each individual is a fixed person, is a stubbornly held (but illusory view) that tends to cause great and unnecessary suffering. This is because it makes us feel isolated and disempowered – incapable of releasing our stubborn opinions, or of entering into proper dialogue with others, with whom we share our essential humanity.

A helpful illustration is sometimes used to advantage in Indian spirituality. It likens individual people to separate waves, composed of nothing else but water that belongs to the wider ocean. In just the same manner as this, the timeless reality of the universe penetrates time-bound matter; time and eternity thus combine in our dual human nature, but there is no contradiction in that – we truly belong to what is universal, while continuing to lead our personal and apparently separate lives as normal.

29

Vision of Wholeness

When you no longer shrink back from fear – when you are no longer afraid of being afraid and dislike yourself for it – then, and only then, anything is possible. This is because it is fear, which is the chief impediment to deep understanding, but when that primary hindrance begins to shift and dissolve, a previously unknown and most wonderful sense of freedom can come to us.

That freedom is nothing new; it is our birth-right, but it is a liberty that does need to be claimed by clear recognition – otherwise it will have no power to act in our experience.

It takes a special kind of courage to face fear. It is by no means easy, and it is wrong to pretend otherwise, but when we dare to approach fear, and then risk everything to encircle it with our warm regard, just as a loving mother might embrace a young child, something surprising can happen.

The sharp sting of fear may be disarmed then by the warmth of our concern. Our kindness is the antidote to fear's venom, while its sting is made safe by our insight, which even allows us to feel some compassion for the unpleasant, darkness of fear, which has held us in thrall for so long.

It is a revelation to discover, as we dare to probe further and deeper, that the raw fear we so often experience, is crying out for love and reassurance – this above all else. Similarly, even the darkest thought-form of fear, is susceptible to the radiant out-reach of this surprising sense of deep caring. That capacity to care for oneself and others, comes to us as a saviour, whenever each new moment of anxiety surges up to cause distress.

Never again need we feel totally abandoned to terror – that is what we find out to such great relief in these dire moments. Fear seldom disappears once and for all overnight, but its days of holding us hostage are numbered.

The acute anxiety that fear engenders, signifies an instinctive dread, not only of the unknown, but also of nothingness itself – and ultimately annihilation. It arises from a deeply-rooted sense of separation from the wholeness of life and strangely enough, we have become painfully accustomed to this sense of separation, because we know of no better.

It is, in fact, the very basis of a false and fragile sense of identity, the veracity of which most of us have never seen fit to challenge, because hardly anybody else does. We have all tended to take for granted the inexorable fact that we are destined to live and die as separate individuals. Death presides over everything, casting a dark shadow, which one does one's level best to ignore.

This is the normal version of what living entails – and yet there is no good reason why anyone should remain bound to this outlook forever. An alternative view, pointing to freedom of mind and soul, is always waiting there in the background – requiring just a slight shift of perspective to become visible.

* * *

Unexpectedly one morning a few years ago, as I paused between serving customers in the small health shop where I worked, there appeared before me a brief window of opportunity to make that critical move – and to change forever the way I regarded myself and the outer world.

I happened to pick up a book on positive thinking, shelved amongst a few similar titles included in the stock, and began to idly leaf through its pages. The work was deceptively simple, but it soon put me straight about that; just a few moments were needed before a passage leapt straight out of a page to grab my attention.

I suddenly perceived, by seeming chance, a clear centre of awareness within myself. It was a place – unmoving and pristine

– untouched by the continual flow of thoughts and images generated by the mind. I saw then and there – plain as day – that there was a simple choice to be made. Either I could identify with the background of stillness, or stubbornly continue to side with the passing thoughts and sensations that had always brought so much anxiety in the wake of their continual ups and downs.

This was the distinct alternative the author, Richard Carlson had just set before me in his remarkable book, *Stop Thinking & Start Living – Common-sense strategies for discovering lifelong happiness.*

In that surprising moment of absolute clarity, I made the spontaneous decision to stand firm on the unmoving ground of my inmost awareness. The next second, all conflict immediately vanished, and the die was cast. I felt a natural sense of ease and belonging – at one with my surroundings and finally undivided within myself. I was *taken* by silence – drawn into deep silence – and in the light of that direct and immediate perception, there was simply no need whatever to feel desolate or isolated any longer. It was, in fact, impossible to do so.

Truly this was illumination - a *vision of wholeness* - a perception that has remained present ever since to utterly transform my outlook. This was the breakthrough I had long been awaiting. For years I had suffered from the inescapable sense of a painful blockage within my consciousness, which I had felt powerless to dissolve – but now for no apparent reason, it had melted away by itself, as if it had never existed.

I cannot adequately describe the relief I felt, but it was enormous. I could have shouted out for joy, had it been appropriate to do so in a shop setting. It was clearly not the time or place for that – and so I was obliged to turn instead to the lyrical stumbling of free verse to express immediately in a few lines what normal words could never say in full. It was a poor substitute, but it was better than nothing:

Honour the body, the cycles of the body, the structure, the reality and substance... welcome this fundamental feeling, the sweetness... surrender to the origin of the mystery that can never be touched or understood... it belongs to you, to your essence. Let us be taken by what is natural within us...

It is certain that in unguarded moments, countless other people must have glimpsed this amazing fact that their true being is boundless – without end and beyond the constraints of time. Yet it is probable too that they have not dared talk openly about such a curious but familiar feeling, in case they are derided. Still perhaps now times have changed in favour of greater transparency – so we no longer need to fight shy of speaking out according to our deepest convictions.

The rewards of candour far outweigh the risks of not being taken seriously in a world of safe conventions. It does not matter what anyone else thinks – if for once someone clearly experiences the natural lightness of their own being, the heavy weight of mortality will never again feel quite such a burden, or their life seem quite so sombre. I can guarantee that.

In truth, the state of being free from fear is the most normal thing in the world. Fear is simply a bad habit, which will begin to leave us as soon as we realise it is unnecessary. What remains is gladness, pure and simple, together with an emboldened curiosity to discover what the remainder of our life may hold – now it has been freed from the cruel fetters of a divided consciousness.

30

Living in Beauty

At the close of each day, pause awhile and give thanks for the fleeting hours that have only just gone – whether they have been easy or difficult, happy or sad. Count your blessings anyway as you quietly consider how your life will have counted for little if you have not frequently felt grateful for the unceasing beauty of the world.

And if you are mostly so absorbed by the endless demands of living that all too often you fail to notice the wonders of Nature all around you, do not pass judgement on yourself, but instead bring compassion to bear on the suffering of others – more bereft of background support than you have ever been.

When the individual misery of human life is left unchecked and multiplied many times, the consequences go a long way to account for the great sorrow we see in society at large. And that is an unfortunate fact for which we must each take a measure of responsibility, because the outer world reflects the quality of our own life. It is an extension and expression of our own consciousness.

Yet there is no room for blame, no need for harsh judgement concerning the way things happen to be. Living inconspicuously behind the scenes as so many of us are obliged to do, still we can accomplish a great deal through our own unassuming example of courage in adversity. It is better by far to do what we can to help, while we can, than waste valuable time in regret for what might have been, if things had only been done differently.

To live with clear-sighted wisdom in a world freshly perceived in the illumined perspective of its essential unity, is the resumption of normality at the deepest level. To be able to view the ordinary mess of human affairs with more clarity and hope – and in the light of an active faith renewed through deep understanding – is good enough reason to rejoice, is it not?

We need to celebrate the simple fact we are still alive and reasonably well – notwithstanding the difficulties that will inevitably remain, so long as our physical existence endures. It is quite normal to feel happy, normal to experience joy. Living is not intended to be a miserable affair, beset by problems and conflict. It is only humanity's collective ignorance that has made it so.

We cannot control our individual destiny and some hardship is inevitable, because of the enhanced instability of an earth in ecological crisis. Yet when through the clarity of higher reasoning, you are enabled to view life as undivided in its totality, suffering immediately diminishes and peace increases. This then could be the true purpose of authentic spiritual practice – to live with love, conscious of oneness and deeply aware of beauty. It is wonderful to even *try* to live in that way – and one is naturally grateful for the opportunity to do so.

* * *

What does it really mean to 'live in beauty' – and why is gratitude so essential at every twist and turn of the path? To continue daily life, alert to the promptings of beauty is to live without expectation and free of the barrier of a strong self-image. To remain grateful for beauty in its manifold forms, allows us to take life as it comes, patient despite its ceaseless demands upon our energy and goodwill; it means ensuring we utilise our native skills of intelligence, discernment and common sense to resolve conflicts and misunderstandings as they arise.

Above all, to live in beauty requires us to live with kindness and without despair – never losing sight of life's inherent sanctity. Awareness of beauty implies all these things, while gratitude for the ceaseless blessings that living affords, takes us directly to the deep stillness that always dwells at the heart of life itself – and within us too.

We are touched by beauty through our innate sensitivity, which will never allow life's rich abundance to be taken for granted. And if all this sounds rather like a counsel of perfection – off the scale of anyone's reasonable list of good resolutions – rest assured that the cultivation of virtues, which we are attempting, is no ordinary undertaking. Any goodness that accrues to our credit here on earth, comes from Heaven – and is not our immediate concern.

The cherishing of fine qualities is a valuable spiritual practice, but such an endeavour has little to do with the attainment of anything. Fundamental virtue gives rise to wisdom and integrity, but we can never call those beautiful attributes our own – either to grasp them or to hold them fast.

We should do the right thing simply because it is right – and love for love's sake too – but not for any other reward. Simple goodness cares not to know that it is good. Yet even so, those uplifting qualities that are the wonderful outcome of goodness, are made much more possible in our experience, when we deeply understand the universal principles of harmony that govern the universe.

As the Bible proclaims, God is the bearer of all good things and the bringer of concord. All we can contribute for our part, is do the best we can in all circumstances and remain grateful for small mercies. Anything else we need will surely be added unto us.

Part Four

Making Sense of the Search

31

The Bottom Line

Difficulties most definitely bring out the best in people – and how instructive it is for us to notice that fact. Truly – it is inspiring to behold the surprisingly courageous manner with which so many people face up to adversity, while for others, critical situations serve differently to summon up the finest of firm qualities within them. Their nobility of character is revealed through a quiet refusal to betray their highest ideals.

We see from these examples how everyone needs to have a bottom line when a firm stance should be taken, regarding vital issues of ethics and human rights. But for spiritual devotees, whose conscious experience has been touched by the radiance of the inner light, there are other considerations that cannot be brushed aside.

The increased clarity we have found, regarding the fundamental principles of universal harmony, brings with it the onus of greater responsibility for the way we conduct our life. We can no longer behave in a reprehensible way, heedless of the consequences. Nobody in any case, can hope to evade karma – the Indian term for the unalterable law of cause and effect, but the results of wrong actions are intensified when one has made the definite choice to follow a spiritual path.

Yet there is no good reason for despair. If a measure of faith has already come to us – and we take good care of the tender shoots of its inconspicuous growth – we will surely be accorded a measure of protection from outer impacts. It is in accordance with God's loving mercy that this should be so.

Most valuable of all perhaps, will be an increasing inclination to trust in the basic goodness of life. Courage, tenacity and trust – these are cardinal qualities to be particularly prized on the path to Truth. And so above all, it is vital that we cherish this dawning sense of quiet confidence in the profound spiritual teachings we may have been fortunate enough to absorb during our long journey inwards to find the source of our own being.

As we value any helpful guidance we have received – and try to put it into practice – our perseverance will be rewarded by an enhanced awareness of the potent veracity of the sound principles, which underlie our practice. The positive qualities of discernment and wisdom that emerge from natural goodness, may appear unassuming at first sight, but they underpin a virtuous kind of life, which is highly conducive to harmony and peace.

* * *

The central claim of the ancient mystical traditions of the world is unequivocal: that there is a higher Power – and that it *is* sacred. But for the earnest devotee, who has already taken this teaching to heart, it soon becomes natural also to take seriously their own intuitive judgement, concerning the essential unity of all created things. It is no longer a far-out notion in the realm of speculation for them, but it has become a living fact with the power to transform experience.

That direct and immediate apperception – moment by moment – that we *belong* to the universe and that therefore none amongst us can be separate from its totality, forms the very foundation of a personal faith, that can also be regarded as universal. Mystics further believe, not only that supreme power is intrinsically sacred by virtue of its omnipresent, omniscient and omnipotent nature, but also that everything is enfolded in its providential care, down to the smallest detail.

The age-old question of how a merciful God can permit evil to flourish, has no casual answer. But it simply cannot be correct to suggest that evil proves the non-existence of God, or that our

Creator is heedless – oblivious of the sufferings of His creatures – and therefore not entirely benign. We need to be prepared to move beyond this superficial view – to look deeper to establish our own convictions, regarding the inscrutable potency of divine love, which must be beyond all worldly understanding.

It is important to keep an open mind as we traverse all obstacles on the spiritual journey. And one more discovery is helpful in enabling one to proceed calmly and steadily down the path of Self-knowledge. It seems that only when one is willing to take risks in pushing one's boundaries, does an innate capacity for trust reveal itself.

When we insist on hanging back from meeting new challenges and play safe, our horizons shut down, but when we go forward in faith, fresh courage and strength are given to us. Over time, heartening insights to encourage us along the way, spontaneously arise. Bit by bit, we gradually learn to let go of our habitual resistance to the inevitable difficulties of daily living.

Whenever we dare to face our deepest fears, our heart opens in consequence. We become open to the inflow of pure love, which unfailingly brings fortitude. It is a profound love that belongs to the essence of our being, but which is readily veiled by anxiety or doubt.

The rewards are immense if we can only take these crucial first steps towards nurturing a wholesome way of living. It is a creative approach to life in which a basic attitude of trust is taken as normal, while we do not forget to exercise sensible discernment whenever necessary. As we proceed to lay this natural foundation of virtue in an unassuming way, we will develop integrity without self-consciousness or undue effort. By this point, we ourselves will have become trustworthy and capable of the fidelity of unfeigned affection.

We need not ponder these things unduly, but by now we will most certainly have already found a good measure of happiness and peace. Is that not what we have always needed and wanted most earnestly?

At last we may feel convinced that we are heading in the right direction – yet even at this point it is crucial that we remain mindful of the unfathomable mystery of life. And in this respect, of course, the great beauty of Nature offers a ready reminder of the sacred – while we make sure to keep our remembrance alive, infused by prayer or clarified by meditation.

Progress is assured, so long as we look to our integrity – that should always be the main priority. Then we will gradually become capable of deriving real benefit from even the sternest of tests – and in this manner we will see how our trust in spiritual practice has become firmly founded. Taking a stand on the truth of our immediate experience, helps us to see clearly what it means to live to the full – and with steady practice we become inwardly resilient, without realising exactly how this has happened.

Gaining resolve in mindfulness, we will more easily be able to maintain a conscious connection with our true being in all circumstances. We are finally ready to be of real service to the world. Yet in many respects, any transformation in our outlook is nothing special, so nothing much has changed – at least on the surface. Perhaps, nevertheless, we are more clearly conscious than ever before of the direction and true purpose in life – and that is surely quite enough.

32

A Hill Held as Sacred

To look for God ignoring Thee who art Being and Consciousness is like going with a lamp to look for darkness. Only to make Thyself known as Being and Consciousness, Thou dwellest in different religions under different names and forms. If yet they do not come to know Thee, they are indeed the blind who do not know the Sun. Oh Arunachala the great! Thou peerless Gem, abide and shine Thou as my Self, One without a second!

**Wise guardian of universal faith – the Sage of Arunachala,
Sri Ramana Maharshi, as photographed by Swiss travel writer,
Ella Maillart.**

To reflect deeply upon the spirit of a place in acknowledgement of the great power it commands – as this Tamil hymn of praise does with impassioned devotion – is to approach the inscrutable mystery that the ancient hill of Arunachala represents.

There are many places of spiritual potency in the world, but this most noble of outcrops – standing out amongst many lesser hills upon the arid plains of South India – has an aura of such radiance that it cannot easily be ignored or forgotten.

Just as darkness flees before the light of the rising sun, so this unique, rugged landscape – often celebrated in Indian stanzas like this one for its invisible potency – does indeed appear to have immense power to absorb the impenetrable darkness of ignorance.

For many visitors, fortunate enough to walk upon its rocky slopes or even view it from afar, Arunachala dwells as a mysterious terrain with a magnetic aura that seems to act incisively to clarify perplexity and ease the tangled knots of mind and heart.

At any rate, I have found it has undoubtedly done so in my own experience – and throughout this book I have endeavoured to write as best I can about the profound, long-term implications of such spiritual transformation, which for me was initiated in its vicinity.

This is no small matter. Such strange and subtle things need to be experienced at first-hand to be believed. Only when our faith is tested and ennobled by adversity does it grow stronger and more stable, but the penetrating influence of a sacred place can undoubtedly support and quicken the winnowing process of purification that belongs to any spiritual path.

The quest for authentic spiritual truth rates amongst the finest of aspirations, but it still needs to remain earthed in practical affairs if it is to retain enduring value amidst the challenging demands of daily life.

In the light of such a common sense observation, it seems entirely appropriate that the reflections in this book, about deep-acting spiritual practices like Self-inquiry and mindfulness, should begin and end, framed by descriptions of an actual location – a majestic place not only long held to be sacred, but also grounded in physical reality.

It is not without good reason that ancient pilgrimage sites such as Arunachala have always been regarded as providing a vital link between Heaven and earth. Yet honouring that sacred link must – as an absolute imperative – include tacit recognition of practical necessities in daily living.

Our earnest efforts to make progress on the spiritual path must always remain grounded in a tangible situation that the world at large can readily verify. Anything less would be to court delusion, making it almost impossible for us to function normally in daily life.

It has been the main task of my life to find this equipoise, without which the most well-meaning spiritual efforts would have failed to deliver genuine happiness or peace – and would in consequence have been to no real avail either for myself, or for anyone else.

* * *

It turned out that circumstances would not permit me to stay on in India, after I had first gone there for that prolonged period in my youth. After nearly four years away, I had anyway become restless to return home to England to put into practice what I had learnt. Finding work, as well as integrating my fresh understanding with daily life, would evidently be the crucial next steps – but the process of adapting once again to life in the West would not prove straightforward.

I was in no position to stipulate the conditions I would find, but I would instead simply need to entrust myself to Providence. It was a case of exchanging a safe-haven for an unknown future, exposed to the unforgiving pressures of a heedless world – and bereft of the support of a spiritual community where I had found many new friends of like-mind. I was full of new-found enthusiasm – but my confidence would soon be dented.

Many years of turbulence were to follow. But when eventually I did manage to return to this special part of India, after so long away, I came with a very different attitude – displaying an outlook no less reverential, but one rendered altogether more realistic by adversity.

Having largely lost touch with Indian culture in the meantime, I had somehow come back with few expectations on this occasion, and yet upon arrival, never had this beautiful hill seemed more majestic in appearance or magnetic in its atmosphere.

* * *

Arunachala is invariably associated nowadays with the great Hindu sage, Ramana Maharshi. When as a youth of just seventeen, Sri Ramana gained full realisation of the deathless spirit within him, it was to this place – revered as sacred since antiquity – that he immediately came as a liberated, young renunciate.

Later in life, the Master composed a series of devotional hymns to Arunachala – and the two enigmatic verses chosen to open the Prologue and Epilogue were both written by him.

Having forsaken kith and kin, Ramana was never inclined to leave his new abode, and gradually a community of devotees formed around him. It was at the ashram founded on this unique spot where I too was most fortunate to be able to stay for an extended period.

This peerless *Sad-Guru* of resplendent qualities had passed away twenty years previously, but many of his direct disciples were still living there. I found them to be not only wise but more than glad to communicate the Maharshi's profoundly direct message to young Western visitors, who, like myself, all tended to arrive eager to receive authentic spiritual guidance.

Upon my return to the ashram more than 40 years after I had left, I could not help but look back upon my life with gratitude.

I found adequate time and space then to properly recall the manifold difficulties I had undergone over the years, while marvelling at the far-reaching changes in my outlook – and how much happier I now felt than ever before.

I reflected how it was almost half a century earlier – on the very first night I had slept in the tranquil hermitage, nestling at the foot of Arunachala – that I had experienced an electrifying dream. That powerful dream had made it abundantly clear to me what potent spiritual forces were present and active there in that highly charged location – and it was made freshly evident to me on my latest visit that nothing has changed in that respect.

It will always be a tremendous blessing to remain for a while in Bhagavan's peaceful abode – but that does not mean anyone will necessarily be spared the fierce pains of spiritual awakening. In order to grow in spiritual maturity, one needs to sacrifice something of oneself – there is no other way to move on decisively.

The shattering dream that had come unbidden so long ago occurred as I slumbered in the ashram compound – exhausted after the long journey from England. It awoke me abruptly with a start, only for my body and mind to be immediately overwhelmed by fear and panic.

In these first anguished seconds of being roused, it seemed as if a tightly-coiled spring of tension deep within me had been unleashed as I slept. The sense of agitation was so acute when I awoke that I even felt that an unbearable state of madness had overtaken me.

God help me! What could I do – where could I turn? A torrent of agonising thoughts engulfed me. And then, as quickly as it had come, the terror and agitation had vanished. Something unimaginably terrible had left me in those dreadful moments. I felt deeply shaken – but what an immense relief it was to be free of that unknown burden.

A curse had been lifted perhaps – or a dark karmic stain had been erased. It certainly felt like that, but who can say exactly what this experience signified? In any case, it was a deep initiation of some kind and was a clear intimation of a more abundant life to come.

Arunachala had granted me a blessing of great power on my very first visit – but with it came an undoubted responsibility to dedicate the remainder of my life in service to the Supreme. It is this higher power that has both created the universe – and may see fit to sustain it in its providential care until the end of time. Words – more words. It is best to remain silent.

* * *

In its inscrutable way, the ancient hill had summoned me to its foot once again after many years away – but I knew all too well I would soon have to take my leave. I was convinced also that every moment spent in Arunachala's vicinity was precious and felt determined not to waste this special opportunity, which might never come again.

Hour after hour – by night and by day, and again deep into the following night – after the beacon of light had been kindled on the summit, the vast river of humanity continued to flow around the perimeter of the sacred peak – as pilgrims of all ages, castes and creeds completed the eight-mile *pradakshina* to claim their well-earned blessings from Lord Shiva.

But by the time I emerged from the guesthouse to walk the short distance down the high-road to the ashram in the cool of early morning, the flow of pilgrims had dwindled to a trickle. A few buses rumbled past the stragglers, while stray dogs nosed the piles of litter on the road – flotsam and jetsam left after the tide of humanity had receded.

The vast throng of pilgrims had all but dispersed at the end of the great annual feast of *Deepam*. All that remained was a vast stillness pervading an atmosphere that had previously been so alive with constant movement. It was something quite remarkable – a spreading silence altogether more strikingly vibrant than the usual restful quiet of the early hours before the burning sun rose upon another hot day in the Indian winter season.

Postscript

This Indwelling Life

What finally is this indwelling life that wells up as a vibrant and undeniable awareness of being? What is the true nature of this mysterious consciousness that informs, sustains and provides us with the joy and vigour to continue an uneven path to an unknown destination?

All tracks up a mountainside lead ultimately to the summit. All queries concerning the many and varied approaches to truth, reduce and return in the end to silence – to the central inquiry into the origin of existence.

Having asked that primary question about our real identity, we need to allow it then to work its magic, acting like a leaven in dough to transmute our doubts into certainty – to transform the darkness of ignorance into the light of increasing wisdom.

Unconcerned by persistent worries that will not readily yield to our inquiring mind, we just need to stay still and listen to our inwardness – waiting in patience, alert to not-knowing and content not to know if necessary. Who am I – truly and deeply? What essentially is the nature of my being? The language of traditional Christianity is very different to that of Hinduism – but its central truth remains the same. 'Be still and know that I am God.' Our life is not truly ours – it is God's life in us that lives.

The essential point is that God is alive within us – and when we clearly recognise this fundamental fact, everything becomes sacred in our experience. It is then that spiritual practice – undertaken with goodwill and infused with the light of clear comprehension – enables us to become established in the certainty that Life Itself *is* supremely good. God is not different from Love, either, and this conviction marks the dawning of a quiet but unassailable faith.

Epilogue

The Way Just Travelled

Glad to be back – the author upon his return visit to India in 2017.

When I look back to consider how diverse are the threads now woven into the fabric of experience, I can only marvel at the simple beauty of the finished cloth. That richly embroidered tapestry held in memory, will serve perhaps as a lasting reminder of my own extraordinary journey – or stand simply as a fitting analogy for the spiritual quest that countless other seekers have undertaken.

It was the kindly old astrologer, living next door to my room in the ashram compound at the foot of Arunachala, who seemed to understand such matters best – and could plainly foretell what might come to pass. He had been an astute lawyer by profession, and so he was probably just the right person to teach one how to read someone's character merely by looking at their face.

As we studied together a photographic portrait of the English mystical author, Evelyn Underhill, on the dust-wrapper of a volume borrowed from the ashram library, he indicated how each of her eyes held quite a different expression from the other to reveal an unsuspected aspect of her disposition; her two eyes could be studied in turn, simply by occluding the opposite side of her face with one's hand.

It was a revealing exercise and I recall it now in affectionate recollection of my neighbour's calm and measured tone, and with appreciation for the considered advice he always freely offered me when I most needed it. That incident reminds me too that there was something else significant about Evelyn Underhill: how ironic it was that it was there in distant India that I had first encountered this most thoughtful and articulate of writers – the first religious figure to make Christianity at all intelligible for me.

Here was an unusually perceptive Christian guide – steady but certainly not staid. In addition, this eminently sensible Anglican was of an ecumenical persuasion, and could definitely be trusted. Clearly something of a mystic too, Evelyn Underhill could now join the shortlist of acceptable Christian authors I had begun after I first heard about the American Trappist monk, Thomas Merton, with whom I had also felt immediate kinship.

Just like me, Merton had been strongly drawn to Eastern spirituality and similarly had been born of rather unconventional parents who were not regular church-goers. But that was the least of it – there were other parallels altogether more striking and poignant. Both of our mothers had died relatively young; Merton was just a child of six at the time and I had barely turned 21, when I had to suffer that most terrible of bereavements for any young man on the threshold of adulthood.

Merton was born in 1915 – one year on from my mother – and he died unexpectedly in Thailand, on a long journey through

Asia, far away from his monastery of Gethsemani in Kentucky. It was the month of December when his accidental death by electrocution had occurred in 1968 at a religious conference, just a few days before my mother lost her own pitiable battle against cancer in a London hospital.

Life does not stop. I was soon to add to my growing list of alternative-minded Christian teachers, the name of Henry Hamblin, an obscure English mystic whose writings I had also first encountered in the ashram library. Hamblin's teaching legacy was inherited by the gifted Nature poet Clare Cameron, who had succeeded him as Editor *of The Science of Thought Review;* that was the title of a monthly magazine, which he had founded in 1921 to honour the central truth to be found in all the great world religions – while always putting Christianity to the fore.

It was Clare who had later introduced me to the prolific writings of a remarkable Anglican priest, Martin Israel, who had begun his professional life as a Jewish doctor in South Africa, before moving to London, appalled by the racist policies of apartheid; he had subsequently converted to Christianity before entering the priesthood – and my wife and I were married by him in 1980. I was subsequently drawn to write biographical studies of both Clare Cameron and Martin Israel – both issued by my present publishers in 2013 and 2016 respectively.

* * *

As a young man, I had been attracted by the thoughtful philosophic novels of Aldous Huxley, Hermann Hesse and Nevil Shute. But in due course, I would be drawn to read more historic works of wise counsel by Christian authors that my mentors had recommended – inspiring figures like Jean-Paul de Caussade and Jean-Pierre Grou – both great French contemplatives, of the eighteenth century.

Yet even by then, I had already undergone a phase of heartfelt devotion to the young French nun, Saint Therese of Lisieux, who had died in Normandy from tuberculosis in September of 1897, aged just 24. Therese had made a deep impression on me with the firm gentleness of her 'little way' and I had been deeply struck by her remarkable fortitude in the face of great suffering. I had visited her simple Carmelite convent in Normandy several times and had found the tranquil atmosphere there familiar, as previously – before I left on my Indian travels – I had encountered Catholicism during weekend stays at several Roman Catholic monasteries in England and Scotland.

I had found in those cloisters the same definite sense of homecoming – a sign perhaps that my inward path to an authentic faith was being revealed gradually in all its uniqueness. I was not yet fully aware of the unfolding pattern, but bit by bit, my horizons were being extended and my inward vision clarified; more and more pieces of the puzzle were falling into place.

Despite the sense of serenity and glad resilience the young saint's example had evoked in me, I had not yet called off the search for certainty at this point – and I remained restless, while always open to further inspiration. It seemed part of a natural progression that the twentieth-century, Christian Orthodox monk, Staretz Silouan, of Mount Athos, should then come up to claim my ardent attention. It was evident that I still needed a distinct focus for my devotions and had not yet found peace.

The time had now come for me to explore Christianity in this more unfamiliar guise, as I ventured on the pilgrim trail to the Russian Orthodox Monastery of Panteleimon in Greece, where the devout, Silouan had dwelt until his death in 1938. It was there on the shore overlooking the sparkling Aegean that this humble peasant monk had been afforded a vision of Christ and had found blessed relief from his interior trials in the uncreated light of God. In due course, he was to be made a saint in the Eastern Orthodox monastic tradition.

I felt overjoyed to be able to stay for even a few days in that quiet, sunlit place – because it allowed me to sense for myself the profound sense of peace which pervaded the monastery grounds, where Saint Silouan had lived out his days.

That memorable visit and subsequent stays at other monasteries situated amidst the rugged terrain of Mount Athos belonged to my insistent quest for mystical illumination; contemplative teachings were those that most deeply attracted me – while I have never felt fully at ease in the mainstream of Christianity.

* * *

It is noteworthy, but perhaps not so surprising that the figure of Jesus Christ has touched me most deeply – not through biblical texts – but through the heartfelt Lutheran cantatas of J.S. Bach. I know I cannot be the only non-churchgoer who has felt moved to greater faith through the transformative genius of this great composer.

Love and devotion are the keynotes of Bach's beautiful music – and love is also the primary influence that pervades the prophetic writings of Peter Deunov, an inspired Christian teacher of the Perennial Wisdom, from Bulgaria, who died there in 1943.

I only came across extracts from his incisive teachings, as I was undertaking the final revisions of this manuscript, but I found his penetrating wisdom deeply affecting – and those prophetic insights must have altered the tone of my final chapters for the better, even as they have uplifted my own thoughts.

I have chosen a quotation from Peter Deunov – also known as Beinsa Douno – to open this book, because I feel that his instructive words are vested with a special power of blessing. A volume of his collected writings is included in my list of suggested reading – and also mentioned is a title by an eminent Bulgarian disciple of his – Omraam Mikhael Aivanhov.

It must be becoming obvious from my exhaustive description of diverse influences that I have undertaken the most extensive course imaginable in the study of comparative religion. It is something of a miracle how I have managed to sample so many sacred traditions, with hardly any pause – and in tireless quest of their essence. Yet finally – after more than half a century in search of what is true – I have at last come full circle and returned gladly to the Christian fold of my birth with no reservations.

And I have done so knowingly, without the uneasy sense of confinement, which had caused me so much discomfiture in the past and had prompted me to seek elsewhere for meaningful answers. There is no question that I am glad to be back where I belong – reunited with my cultural roots and renewed in a more realistic faith.

I regard my approach to Truth as unconventional nonetheless – it is a spirituality that emerges from Christianity in glad acceptance of suffering and redemption through God's love, but it does so in the most universal sense of what authentic faith implies. The mere attempt to chart different stages on the path has shown, not only how many twists and turns there have been along the way, but also how there is nothing predictable about the process of spiritual awakening. The ascent to Truth will always remain a mystery – different for each one of us and altogether out of our hands.

What is certainly evident from the varied and profound spiritual teachings I have encountered, is that my vocation has retained at its contemplative core, the demanding task of synthesis. I have absorbed a host of uplifting influences over the years, to invite inevitable confusion at times. But, nevertheless, clarity has always prevailed. I have never entirely lost sight of my spiritual bearings, or completely lost touch with an underlying awareness of blessing.

* * *

The exploration of mystical Christianity has run parallel with my deep interest in Eastern religions. I have referred in these pages mostly to Hinduism and Buddhism – but my attention has also been engaged from time to time by Taoism and Judaism, along with the Sufi teachings of mystical Islam.

Over a period of four years, I travelled widely in India and encountered all manner of yogis and adepts - holy men and women, both wise and outlandish. Back in England, it was the late great Sufi master, Hazrat Inayat Khan, who had first opened my eyes to the pellucid beauty of Islamic mystical thought, but my own Sufi teacher in London was to be Irina Tweedie, a forthright and resolute Russian woman, who had documented her traditional training with a stern Indian teacher in vivid diary entries. Mrs Tweedie's reflections make stark reading and she fashioned them into an absorbing book on Sufism, which stands as an invaluable record of authentic spiritual practice of the most rigorous kind.

I still regard Ramana Maharshi as my original Guru, but involvement as a young man with devotees of that highly-regarded Indian sage was just the first phase of my spiritual journey; it was followed by a period of close contact with adherents of the unorthodox Indian teacher, J. Krishnamurti, who had abruptly broken away from all spiritual traditions.

It was the impassioned Krishnamurti, with whom I spoke briefly several times both in India and in England, who was instrumental in widening my horizons to embrace the concerns of a troubled world; he made me aware of a deeper kind of learning offered by a holistic approach to education, which offers long-term hope for the uplift and enlightenment of society.

I initially encountered Buddhism on my youthful travels in North India and many years later was to join for a time the extensive sangha of the Vietnamese Buddhist monk, Thich Nhat Hanh. I found him to be quietly-spoken but immensely sagacious; simply through the gentle but penetrating power of compassion, he provided invaluable support at a particularly difficult stage in my ongoing struggle for clarity and steadiness.

Hard to believe that it was a good 25 years earlier that I had met the German Buddhist scholar, Lama Govinda, when I visited his remote hermitage in the foothills of the Himalayas.

It may have been Thich Nhat Hanh, who had nurtured a deeper appreciation of mindfulness, but it was Lama Govinda, whose uplifting influence and clear interpretation of Tibetan Buddhist teachings had introduced me to its practice and first established the firm foundations of my continuing interest in this profoundly effective form of meditation; I am relieved to find now that the value of mindfulness - the benefits of which both Lama Govinda and Thich Nhat Hanh always extolled - is at long last being increasingly recognised by society here in the West.

During my last visit to India, I covered familiar territory and broke fresh ground too. I was glad to be able to stay for several weeks in Auroville – a vibrant, new-age community near the former French colonial city of Pondicherry – founded by the Aurobindo Mother. She was a remarkable French woman, who became the consort of the enigmatic Indian philosopher, Sri Aurobindo, after he had become involved as a revolutionary in the fierce struggle with the British for Indian independence.

I feel fortunate to have been originally granted an audience with the gracious Mother at her Pondicherry ashram as a young man – two decades after Sri Aurobindo's passing in 1950; I also made on that earlier occasion a first visit to Auroville, which was then at a preliminary stage of its development into the inspiring and viable new-age settlement it has now become. The intense presence of this wise old lady made a profound impression upon me in 1970 – and I still regard her as a powerful spiritual teacher in her own right.

Personal contact with the spiritual guide will always be of the utmost importance on the path, because *darshan* facilitates transmission – the energy of blessing to support the student in the vicissitudes they are bound to encounter.

* * *

I have certainly cast the net of spirituality wide to yield resilience and flexibility of mind over the years – and have no regrets, notwithstanding the various trials and tribulations experienced along the way. I have not been disappointed in my spiritual quest, for I have discovered – despite much turbulence and manifold difficulties – unbounded joy and a good measure of equanimity.

To my surprise, I find myself approaching my latter years without undue anxiety – and to be largely free of such anxiety about old age and the finality of death, is perhaps for me the clearest sign of all that I have changed profoundly. As I seek to sum up the basic attitude of trust in life, which underpins this work, I can do no better than leave the final word to another Western devotee of Ramana Maharshi, who also found glad refuge at his Guru's ashram at the foot of Arunachala on the dusty plains of South India.

'The variety of ways God or the Self brings men to him is amazing to watch,' wrote the elderly Polish writer S.S. Cohen in 1975, in his final book of contemplation on the universal truths of the Vedas.

'No one is forgotten; no one is for ever left behind, and no one is totally annihilated as a "lost soul" for whatever wickedness one has at one time or other been guilty of. The creed of lost souls is not that of the Vedanta: it does not fit in with its teaching of the single Substance, single Existence.'

Acknowledgements

I have not previously placed on record my indebtedness to more than a few good teachers, from whom I have been fortunate to receive detailed spiritual instruction. I gladly do so now, remembering with gratitude the contributions that Hugo Maier, Douglas Harding, John Garrie, Joan Cooper, Irina Tweedie, Peter Goldman and Francis Lucille have made to my understanding and overall welfare.

Here is clearly the place too to thank those of my friends, who have offered sound advice and feedback relating to this new book. My grateful thanks for the care they have taken on my behalf, goes accordingly to the following: Colin Oliver, Chris Quilkey, the Rev. Neil Broadbent, Elizabeth Medler, Stephanie Sorrell, Charles Becker, Muz Murray, Mike Jenkins and Iain Colquhoun. It is easier said than done to remain objective concerning one's own work and so I appreciate the opportunity given to me by fellow writers to hone my skills in this respect.

The photographic portrait of Sri Ramana Maharshi was taken by the intrepid Swiss explorer, Ella Maillart in around 1943. This photo (copyright: succession Ella Maillart et Musee de'L'Elysee, Lausannne) is published by kind permission of Anneliese Hollman and Musee d'Elysee, where her archive is kept.

The two stanzas by Ramana Maharshi, in praise of Arunacala, which are quoted at the beginning of the Prologue and Epilogue, are taken from *Five Hymns to Sri Arunachala*, published by Sri Ramansramam in Tiruvannamalai, South India. Grateful acknowledgement is due to the ashram authorities for their inclusion.

I would finally like to thank the team at John Hunt Publishing for the time and trouble they have taken with production and for generously allowing me extra time to develop the themes contained in this work.

Sources and Suggestions for Further Reading

Aldous Huxley, *The Perennial Philosophy* (London: Chatto & Windus, 1946)

Evelyn Underhill, *Practical Mysticism* (New York: Dover Publications)

Evelyn Underhill, *Letters of Evelyn Underhill,* edited with an Introduction by Charles Williams (London: Longmans, 1956)

Peter Deunov, *Prophet for Our Times*, edited by David Lorimer (London: Hay House, 2015)

Omraam Mikhael Aivanhov *Golden Rules for Everyday Life* (Frejus, France: Editions Prosveta, 1990)

Thomas Merton, *Choosing to Love the World* (Boulder, Colorado: Sounds True, 2008)

Thomas Merton, *The Asian Journal of Thomas Merton* (London: Sheldon Press, 1974)

Jean-Nicholas Grou, *How to Pray* (London: James Clarke, 1955)

Jean-Nicholas Grou, *Manual for Interior Souls* (London: Burns & Oates, 1955)

Jean Pierre de Caussade, *Self-Abandonment to Divine Providence* (London: Burns & Oates, 1962)

Sister Wendy Beckett, *Spiritual Letters* (London: Bloomsbury, 2013)

Archimandrite Sophrony, *The Monk of Mount Athos* (London & Oxford: Mowbrays, 1973)

Robin Amis, *A Different Christianity* (Albany, USA: State University of New York Press, 1995)

Arthur Osborne, *Ramana Maharshi and the Path to Self-Knowledge* (London: Rider 1954)

S.S. Cohen, *Advaitic Sadhana* (Delhi: Motilal Banarsidass, 1975)

Sri Ramana Maharshi, *Talks with Sri Ramana Maharshi* (Tiruvannamalai, India: Sri Ramansramam, 1978)

Thich Nhat Hanh, *The Energy of Prayer* (Berkeley, USA: Parallax Press, 2006)

Lama Anagarika Govinda, *The Way of the White Clouds* (London: Hutchinson, 1966)

Richard Power, *The Lost Teachings of Lama Govinda* (Wheaton, Illinois: Quest Books, 2007)

Jon Kabat Zinn, *Coming to Our Senses* (London: Piatkus, 2013)

Irina Tweedie, *Daughter of Fire* (California, USA: Blue Dolphin Publishing, 1986)

Hua-Ching Ni, *Tao – The Subtle Universal Law and the Integral Way of Life* (Santa Monica, USA: Seven Star Communications, 1979)

Rebbe Nachman of Breslov, *The Empty Chair* (Vermont, USA: Jewish Lights Publishing, 1994)

Richard Carlson, *Stop Thinking & Start Living* (London: Element – HarperCollins, 1993)